's

# Achieving QTLS Status

ditor: Ann Gravells

# Achieving
# QTLS Status

A Guide to Demonstrating the
Professional Standards

## Sharron Mansell

Foreword by
Patricia Odell, Head of QTLS and ATS,
Education and Training Foundation

Learning Matters
An imprint of SAGE Publications Ltd
1 Oliver's Yard
55 City Road
London EC1Y 1SP

SAGE Publications Inc.
2455 Teller Road
Thousand Oaks, California 91320

SAGE Publications India Pvt Ltd
B 1/I 1 Mohan Cooperative Industrial Area
Mathura Road
New Delhi 110 044

SAGE Publications Asia-Pacific Pte Ltd
3 Church Street
#10-04 Samsung Hub
Singapore 049483

Editor: Amy Thornton
Senior project editor: Chris Marke
Project management: Deer Park Productions
Copy editor: Joy Tucker
Proofreader: Caroline Stock
Indexer: Anne Solamito
Marketing manager: Dilhara Attygalle
Cover design: Wendy Scott
Typeset by: C&M Digitals (P) Ltd, Chennai, India
Printed in the UK

**Library of Congress Control Number 2018950476**

**British Library Cataloguing in Publication Data**

A catalogue record for this book is available from
the British Library

ISBN 978-1-5264-6020-2 (pbk)
ISBN 978-1-5264-6019-6

At SAGE we take sustainability seriously. Most of our products are printed in the UK using responsibly sourced
papers and boards. When we print overseas we ensure sustainable papers are used as measured by the PREPS
grading system. We undertake an annual audit to monitor our sustainability.

# CONTENTS

# ACKNOWLEDGEMENTS

We would like to give a special thanks to the following people who have helped us with the production of this book. They have freely given their time, knowledge and advice, which has resulted in some excellent contributions and additions to the content. Without their amazing proof reading skills and honest feedback, this book would not be what it is, and we are truly grateful.

Suzanne Blake – Programme Director – University of Hull

Louise C. Gulbrandsen QTS Med – Teacher – Loavenstad School

Andy Hampel – Lecturer and illustrator – Bishop Burton College

Sue Hosdell MSET, QTLS – Teacher – St Ann's School and Sixth Form College

David Malachi MSET, FCCT, SFHEA, QTLS – Director of Newham College University Centre

Michael Sinanis – Assistant Principal of Corporate Services – White Rose Beauty Colleges

Teresa Thomas – QTLS Operations Director – Education and Training Foundation

Helen Whittle MSET, QTLS, QTS – English Tutor – White Rose Beauty Colleges

Special thanks go to Patricia Odell, Head of QTLS and ATS at the Education and Training Foundation (ETF), for her time, specialist advice and support whilst we were working on the book.

We would like to thank our Senior Commissioning Editor (Education) Amy Thornton for her continued support and guidance.

Every effort has been made to trace the copyright holders and to obtain their permission for the use of copyright material. The publisher, editor and author will gladly receive any information enabling them to rectify any error or omission in subsequent editions.

Ann Gravells
www.anngravells.com

Sharron Mansell
https://www.facebook.com/mansellsharron/

# AUTHOR STATEMENT

**Sharron Mansell**

Sharron started delivering education and training programmes on a part-time basis in 1987, before progressing into a full-time career in further education in 2000. She has gained practical work-based skills and a wide and varied understanding of schools' provision, further and higher education, apprenticeships and full cost courses.

Starting her career as a teacher in a land-based specialist college, she progressed to course management before taking responsibility for several departments within a large further education college. Sharron further developed her knowledge and skills within the sector when her role changed to Head of Services to Business. She is now the Assistant Principal of Quality at the White Rose Beauty Colleges, which is recognised as the UKs largest beauty therapy training provider.

Sharron is passionate about raising standards in education and is committed to supporting quality improvement at all levels and stages. As well as her work in further education and as a Standards Verifier for Pearson, she has also worked with secondary schools as a governor to support quality improvement.

Sharron holds an Honours Degree in Education and Training, has a Certificate in Education, is a Member of the Society for Education and Training, and holds QTLS status.

Although Sharron has been acknowledged for her expertise in reviewing text books, this is the first book she has written. Sharron states she only managed to complete the book due to the help and support from her editor Ann Gravells and the expertise of Patricia Odell, Head of QTLS and ATS at the Education and Training Foundation. In addition, she wishes to express her thanks to Richard, Emma, Steven and Morgan for their continued support.

Sharron can be contacted via:

Facebook: https://www.facebook.com/mansellsharron/
Twitter: https://twitter.com/sharronmansell
LinkedIn: https://www.linkedin.com/in/sharronmansell
Email: sharronmansell@outlook.com

# EDITOR STATEMENT

**Ann Gravells**

Ann has been teaching, assessing and quality assuring in the further education and skills sector since 1983. She is a director of her own company *Ann Gravells Ltd*, an educational consultancy based in East Yorkshire. She specialises in teaching, training, assessment and quality assurance.

Ann holds a Masters in Educational Management, a PGCE, a Degree in Education, and a City & Guilds Medal of Excellence for teaching. She is a Fellow of the Society for Education and Training, and holds QTLS status.

Ann has been writing text books since 2006, which are mainly based on her own experiences as a teacher, and the subsequent education of trainee teachers. She aims to write in plain English to help anyone with their role. She creates resources for teachers and learners such as PowerPoints and handouts for the assessment, quality assurance and teacher training qualifications. These are available via her website: www.anngravells.com

Ann has worked for several awarding organisations producing qualification guidance, policies and procedures, and carrying out the external quality assurance of teaching, assessment and quality assurance qualifications.

She is an Ofqual Assessment Specialist, a consultant to the University of Cambridge's Institute of Continuing Education and a technical advisor to the awarding organisation Training Qualifications UK (TQUK).

Ann welcomes any comments from readers; please contact her via her website www.anngravells.com

# Patricia Odell Head of QTLS and ATS, Education and Training Foundation

Since QTLS was first launched in 2008, over 20,000 practitioners have been awarded with this nationally recognised status. In September 2016 we reformed and strengthened QTLS, so that teachers and trainers can now evidence their progression during the process of professional formation.

Underpinned by the Professional Standards for Teachers and Trainers, QTLS provides a rich developmental opportunity, enabling practitioners to work collaboratively with their supporter as well as their colleagues to improve their practice.

SET members who have gained QTLS tell us that the process has not only helped them to improve their practice, but it has also positively impacted on their learners. Employers are looking for teachers and trainers who are committed to continuing professional development and so undertaking QTLS can enhance career prospects.

Importantly, gaining QTLS sets teachers on the pathway to Advanced Teacher Status (ATS). Launched in 2016, this new status recognises mastery level expertise in experienced teachers and trainers.

I am really pleased to have been able to support Ann and Sharron in ensuring this book accurately reflects the process and that the content is accurate. I am sure this publication will be very helpful to teachers and trainers who are working towards achieving QTLS status.

Congratulations on purchasing this book. It should cover everything you need to know to help you work towards achieving QTLS status through the Society for Education's (SET) professional formation process.

It has been a pleasure to edit this book, written by a long-time colleague of mine: Sharron Mansell. I had always felt a book to help practitioners to gain QTLS status was needed. I couldn't write it as the process has been updated since I originally gained QTLS status. When Sharron telephoned me to say she was going to work towards QTLS, I asked her if she would be interested in writing about it. I felt a book like this needed to be written by someone who was currently going through the process themselves. To my surprise, she said yes.

Both Sharron and I have liaised with SET to ensure the content complements their professional formation process, and we are very grateful for their advice and support.

The book is a guide which will take you from your initial application to completion, with step by step activities linked directly to your workbook. There are tips and activities to assist you through the process which should help you to develop your practice in relation to the Professional Standards.

I hope you discover what you need from the book, I wish you success with gaining QTLS status and I hope you have a wonderful teaching career.

Ann Gravells
www.anngravells.com

# INTRODUCTION

If you are considering undertaking the process of achieving Qualified Teacher Learning and Skills (QTLS) status, and wonder how to go about it, this book is for you. The status is conferred by the Society for Education and Training (SET), of which you will need to be a member.

The book aims to support you through the whole process, known as *professional formation*. This includes your application to become a SET member, registration for QTLS status, how to complete each section of the workbook and how to develop your practice in relation to the Professional Standards.

Although the book has been written for teachers and trainers wishing to achieve QTLS status, it will also provide a valuable resource to refresh the knowledge of those who already hold QTLS status. In addition, the book will aid supporters, mentors, managers and human resource staff in developing their teams' professional values, attributes and motivation for excellence.

Undertaking the process of professional formation to achieve QTLS status is a real benefit to becoming an elite professional. It will give you more confidence, improve your knowledge and skills, and, as a result, have a positive impact on your teaching career, your organisation and your learners.

The topics covered in the book directly relate to SET's workbook and include:

- about you
- role and responsibilities
- self-assessment
- professional development
- continuing professional development record
- critical reflection
- final action plan
- sharing your workbook.

You will find it beneficial to work logically through the chapters. However, you can look up appropriate topics in the index (at the back of the book) to access relevant information.

You can also use the book as a refresher if you have already achieved QTLS status, or if you wish to confirm you are meeting the Professional Standards.

The appendices at the back of the book include the Professional Standards and the list of mandatory evidence which must be provided during the professional formation process. A list of relevant books and websites is available at the end of each chapter to help with your further development.

There are many external weblinks within the book; if you find any which no longer work, please email sharronmansell@outlook.com. Also, if an instruction has changed regarding an activity which relates to the SET workbook, please do get in touch. This will help to update the book for future readers.

# 1
# Background to QTLS

**Introduction**

This chapter will explore the background to Qualified Teacher Learning and Skills (QTLS) status.

It will introduce you to the Professional Standards for Teachers and Trainers in Education and Training in England (hereinafter called the Professional Standards). As a teacher or trainer, you should demonstrate your commitment to them as part of your professional practice, and whilst working towards QTLS status.

It will also guide you regarding what the further education and skills sector is all about, and how the Education and Training Foundation (ETF) can support you.

**This chapter will cover the following topics:**

- What QTLS status is
- The Professional Standards
- The further education and skills sector
- The Education and Training Foundation

# What QTLS status is

QTLS status is a voluntary process which can help you to advance your career. It demonstrates your expertise and experience to colleagues, employers and learners. Having QTLS status shows you are a professional teacher who is committed to their role, and who will carry out continuing professional development (CPD).

QTLS is gained by successfully completing a process known as *professional formation*, which takes approximately four to six months. This process enables you to demonstrate how you are continuing to develop, and apply the skills and knowledge gained from your initial teacher education (ITE) qualification to your current practice. Access to QTLS status is one of the key benefits of being a member of the Society for Education and Training (SET). Underpinned by the Professional Standards, QTLS status will help you to consolidate your existing practice as well as develop new skills and knowledge. SET is the only body that can confer QTLS status.

Undertaking the process of QTLS is a way to stretch and challenge yourself to develop your practice and your subject knowledge. You will be undertaking the process alongside your usual teaching role, therefore you will need to be dedicated and resilient, and have the time to commit to it.

You could think of the professional formation process as a cycle which is based on a self-assessment of your role and what you need to develop. It continues with a plan for your professional development, relevant CPD activities, a critical reflection of what you have done, and ends with a final action plan, as in Figure 1.1. All these aspects will be explained as you progress through the book. The evidence you will need to provide for each is listed in Appendix 2.

**Figure 1.1 The professional formation cycle**

You can only work towards your professional formation once you have achieved a recognised teaching qualification, for example, the Diploma in Education and Training (DET) at Level 5. You need to have been qualified for at least six months. You must currently be teaching learners aged 14 plus (i.e. in years 10, 11 and above) and/or with adults for at least two hours per week. You must be able to evidence your current practice with groups of learners (not just on a one-to-one basis).

**Tip**

*If you teach predominantly on a one-to-one basis, you can still apply for professional formation. However, you must be able to provide current evidence of teaching a group (five or more learners) for at least one of your observed lessons.*

If you are working in a primary school setting, you can't use any evidence of teaching younger learners. However, you may still be eligible if you are involved in a significant amount of family learning activity, i.e. with parents or carers at the school. If you are unsure, contact SET directly; its details are on the website listed at the end of this chapter.

**Activity**

*If you would like to read about SET members' experiences of achieving QTLS status, take a look at the case studies at this link: https://tinyurl.com/ycy6svbq*

## The key benefits of QTLS status

More than 20,000 practitioners have achieved QTLS status since its introduction in 2008.

The key benefits are:

- QTLS status is recognised in law as having parity with Qualified Teacher Status (QTS) for teaching in a maintained school in England

- career progression: QTLS status demonstrates your commitment, skills and knowledge to employers

- recognition of your status as a professional teacher or trainer (you will be added to SET's online professional register)

- valuable CPD opportunities which can build confidence and enhance your knowledge and skills

- using the letters QTLS as a designation after your name

- taking advantage of certain benefits of being a SET member

- the opportunity to apply for Advanced Teacher Status (ATS) as your career progresses.

## Who is it for?

- Teachers, trainers and professionals working in the further education and training sector.

- Qualified Further Education (FE) teachers working as teaching assistants, tutors or instructors in academies, schools or sixth form colleges.

- Teachers or trainers who have recently completed their initial teacher training, as well as those who already have experience of teaching.

# The Professional Standards

The Education and Training Foundation's (ETF) Professional Standards were developed in 2014 in consultation with representatives from the FE and skills sector. They are aimed at teachers and trainers working in the sector (excluding sixth form colleges), who work in a voluntary or a paid capacity. This includes offender institutions, the armed forces, charitable, commercial and any other public sector body and their employees.

> *Teachers and trainers are 'dual professionals'; they are both subject and/or vocational specialists and experts in teaching and learning. They are committed to maintaining and developing their expertise in both aspects of their role to ensure the best outcomes for their learners. These expectations of teachers and trainers underpin the 2014 Professional Standards, with their overall purpose being to support teachers and trainers to maintain and improve standards of teaching and learning, and outcomes for learners.*

https://tinyurl.com/y7x7b5j2 (date accessed 16 July 2018)

The Professional Standards:

- set out clear expectations of effective practice in education and training

- enable teachers and trainers to identify areas for their own professional development

- support initial teacher education

- provide a national reference point that organisations can use to support the development of their staff.

https://tinyurl.com/o2cv9fs

## Activity

*Take a look at the Professional Standards in Appendix 1 to familiarise yourself with them. You will need to refer to them as you progress through the professional formation process.*

The Professional Standards were designed to:

- motivate and enthuse teachers and trainers to take ownership of their own professional development and to perform at their optimum

- demonstrate professionalism through outstanding practice whilst striving to ensure all learners reach their full potential.

There are 20 Professional Standards which relate to three areas:

- *professional values and attributes* – six standards aimed at developing judgement of what works and does not work in your teaching and training

- *professional knowledge and understanding* – six standards aimed at developing deep and critically informed knowledge and understanding in theory and practice

- *professional skills* – eight standards aimed at developing your expertise and skills to ensure the best outcomes for learners.

The Professional Standards are based on fundamental values, attributes, skills, knowledge and understanding. They will enable you to systematically, safely and consistently self-evaluate your own performance, identify your own training needs and contribute to your organisation's quality assurance processes. The Professional Standards will be explained further in Chapter 5.

# The further education and skills sector

The FE and skills sector is comprised of those aged 14 and above. It includes a wide range of vocational and academic practitioners who share their skills and expertise with learners in different environments and contexts, for example:

- adult education
- armed, emergency and uniformed services
- charitable organisations
- community education
- further education colleges
- health authorities
- higher education institutions and universities
- immigration and detention centres
- laboratories
- local authorities
- on site learning centres
- prisoner and offender centres
- private sector learning
- probation services
- public and private training organisations
- schools and academies
- sixth form colleges
- technical colleges
- voluntary sector learning
- work-based learning.

## Activity

*Consider the following questions and make a few notes in response to them.*

- *Why am I a teacher/trainer?*

- *In what environment or context do I teach?*

- *How did I move into the profession?*

- *What is motivating me to be the best I can be?*

*Keep your notes, as you will need to refer back to them as you progress through the professional formation process.*

## Funding in the sector

Funding in the sector can be quite complex. Colleges and sixth form institutes (in England) are funded directly from the government via the Education and Skills Funding Agency (ESFA). A private training provider might deliver education and training by subcontracting from a FE college and may also have a direct contract with the ESFA. Alternatively, some training organisations will charge their learners a fee.

The ESFA is sponsored by the Department of Education, and funding streams include:

- 16–18 Study Programme

- 19+ Loans

- Adult Education Budget (AEB)

- Adult Learning Support (ALS) encompassing Care to Learn and specialist college placement funding for Learners with Learning Difficulties and Disabilities (LLDD)

- Community Provision Learning

- European Social Fund (ESF)

- Job Centre Plus (JCP)

- levy and non-levy apprenticeships

- Offender Learning

- Prince's Trust

- Traineeship

- work-based learning (WBL).

In addition, some learners choose to fund themselves (known as *full cost*) and don't access any ESFA funding. Learners in the sector can access FE from the age of 14, i.e. they could work towards a vocational programme in an organisation other than a school. Further information regarding full-time enrolment of 14–16 year-olds in further education and sixth form colleges can be found at this link: https://tinyurl.com/y866wt2w

There have been many reforms to the FE sector, including the 2013 raising of participation age (RPA) to enable young people to stay in education until their 18th birthday. Each government change tends to bring further modification of the education system. If you are interested in this, further reading regarding the history and reforms in education can be found at this link: https://tinyurl.com/yc348lq9 and key dates can be found at this link: https://tinyurl.com/ya7ojfcs

## Activity

*Find out which funding streams (if any) your learners are accessing and what impact this might have on your organisation – for example, if any learners leave the programme early or if they do not achieve the required qualification.*

## Historical perspective of QTLS

The Institute for Learning (IfL) was the first UK professional body for FE and was incorporated in 2002 as a not for profit body. It was established to maintain quality; standards; and the practice of teaching and learning. Until 2006, membership was voluntary. However, it became compulsory in 2007 as part of the Further Education Teachers' Regulations in England. At this point, the government paid the membership fees and for practitioners to undertake QTLS status. The IfL was recognised as the acting regulatory body for those delivering on behalf of providers who were in receipt of government education funding.

In 2012, the Lingfield Inquiry *Professionalism in Further Education Interim Report* recommended the deregulation of the 2007 Further Education Teachers' Regulations. They were therefore revoked in September 2013, and the IfL repealed the mandatory membership registration to its original voluntary position. QTLS status remained, but on a voluntary basis, and from October 2013 members had to fund it themselves.

In 2014, it was decided to close the IfL and pass all assets to the newly formed Education and Training Foundation (ETF).

## Activity

*If you are interested in the history of IfL, ETF and SET, take a look at these links: https://tinyurl.com/yb8zeaj3 and https://tinyurl.com/ycr2glhk*

The ETF launched its own professional membership service called the Society for Education and Training (SET) in March 2015, where professional practitioners can still apply for QTLS status. Members have legal parity regarding pay and conditions with QTS if they work in a school setting. This is on the condition that they remain a member of SET.

> *If you have QTLS status and membership with the Society for Education and Training, you will be eligible to work as a qualified teacher in schools in England.*
>
> *It will be up to schools and local authorities to decide whether you are suitable for a post and to teach a particular subject. You will be exempt from serving a statutory induction period in schools.*
>
> *https://tinyurl.com/o9xnzfx (date accessed 16 June 2018)*

QTLS status is therefore a recognised professional status which is highly regarded within the sector.

## Activity

*Take a look at the differences between QTS and QTLS at this link: https://tinyurl.com/yb6trzow*

The process of achieving QTLS status was reformed by SET in 2016 in order to:

- be more forward-looking with opportunities to plan and record CPD activities, and to demonstrate progression
- encourage collaborative working with a supporter and other colleagues throughout the process
- give applicants the opportunity to critically reflect on the difference their development activities have had on their practice and their learners
- inspire applicants to continue developing their skills and knowledge after completing the professional formation process.

## Tip

*Throughout the book, there are many links to pages on the ETF and SET websites. These links might change, therefore if a link does not work, just search for the topic via the search box on the SET website.*

*https://set.et-foundation.co.uk/*

# The Education and Training Foundation

The Education and Training Foundation (ETF) was established in October 2013 as a registered charity. It is the government-backed, sector-owned national support body for the FE and skills sector and is the guardian of the Professional Standards.

The ETF's role is to support the continuing transformation of the technical and vocational education system by ensuring the sector has world-class leaders, teachers and trainers. In turn, this leads to ever-improving learner outcomes, provides a better skilled workforce for employers and creates a stronger economy, country and society.

The ETF do this by improving, driving and championing the quality of the sector's leadership, teaching and training through:

- setting and promoting the Professional Standards

- supporting sector change

- leading workforce development for leaders, governors and practitioners

- providing key workforce data and research.

## The Society for Education and Training (SET)

The Society for Education and Training (SET) is the membership service for the Education and Training Foundation (ETF).

*SET is the largest professional membership organisation for teachers and trainers in the UK. SET membership makes you part of a large network of experienced teaching professionals. It offers you professional recognition, unlocks your career potential and helps you to become the best teacher or trainer you can be.*

https://tinyurl.com/ya45at7z (date accessed 16 July 2018)

The ETF (through SET) remains the only body which confers Qualified Teacher Learning and Skills (QTLS) status and Advanced Teacher Status (ATS). ATS will be explained in Chapter 10.

*The key benefits of becoming a member of SET*

Joining SET will give you benefits such as:

- accessing and using the online research library of CPD content and resources

- becoming a mentor or mentee through the ETF's mentoring service

- being a member of the largest professional network of teachers and trainers in the UK

- being listed in the online professional SET register (after gaining QTLS status)

- career advice

- career progression: QTLS status demonstrates your commitment, skills and knowledge to employers; ATS demonstrates you are an experienced professional

- eligibility for discounts on the latest professional development workshops, webinars and courses offered by the ETF

- free confidential legal advice

- meeting with like-minded professionals via local events, an annual conference and/or online communities

- receiving the quarterly copy of *inTuition*, the most widely read journal for those working in post-16 education (digital and hard copy)

- using the letters SET as a designation after your name.

### Corporate Partner status

SET introduced Corporate Partner status in May 2017. This is a status which serves as a badge of recognition to organisations. It shows that an organisation is committed to investing in staff development, progression and high-quality recruitment.

Corporate Partner status enables colleges and independent training providers (ITP) to access the entire suite of services offered by the ETF. This covers a vast range of CPD, practical advice, support and networking opportunities. Alongside this, Corporate Partners are encouraged to motivate their teachers and trainers to achieve QTLS status and ATS.

Benefits include:

- SET partner logo for use on the organisation's website and marketing materials

- discounted SET membership for staff

- use of SET CPD tools and support to integrate into performance development review processes

- access to ETF training courses at discounted rates

- complementary SET membership for one member of the management team, and three copies of SET's journal: *inTuition*

- staff workshops to get maximum value from SET.

The aim of the partnership status is to offer bespoke solutions for colleges and ITPs, and to keep teachers connected to their practice. This ongoing professional development offer for staff can benefit the whole organisation alongside its learners, partners and local employers.

## *Activity*

*Find out if your organisation is a Corporate Partner to the ETF as there may be help within your organisation to work towards QTLS status.*

# Summary

This chapter has explored the background to QTLS status.

It has introduced you to the Professional Standards for Teachers and Trainers in Education and Training in England. As a professional teacher or trainer, you should demonstrate your commitment to them as part of your professional practice and whilst working towards QTLS status.

You might like to carry out further research by accessing the books and websites listed at the end of this chapter.

This chapter has covered the following topics:

- What QTLS status is

- The Professional Standards

- The further education and skills sector

- The Education and Training Foundation

# References and further information

ETF (2014) *Initial Guidance for Users of the Professional Standards.*

Gravells, J. and Wallace, S. (2013) *An A–Z Guide to Working in Further Education.* Northwich: Critical.

Tummons, J. (2014) *A to Z of Lifelong Learning.* Berkshire: OU Press.

Tummons, J. (2010) *Becoming a Professional Tutor* (2nd edition). Exeter: Learning Matters.

# Websites

Advanced Teacher Status (ATS) – https://tinyurl.com/ydhtcjyo

Education and Skills Funding Agency (ESFA) – https://tinyurl.com/mdrltn8

Education and Training Foundation (ETF) – www.et-foundation.co.uk

ETF (2014) Professional Standards for Teachers and Trainers – https://tinyurl.com/o2cv9fs

FE Advice – www.feadvice.org.uk

Key dates in education – https://tinyurl.com/ya7ojfcs

QTLS status – https://tinyurl.com/y86vc3f8

QTLS status case studies – https://tinyurl.com/y9bo2arw

Society for Education and Training (SET) – https://set.et-foundation.co.uk

# 2

# Getting started with the QTLS professional formation process

**Introduction**

Working towards Qualified Teacher Learning and Skills (QTLS) status is known as *professional formation*. There are various processes you will need to go through to get started. This includes becoming a member of the Society for Education and Training (SET) and then submitting your application.

This chapter will explore how to start the professional formation process, how to use your workbook and what happens when you have completed it.

**This chapter will cover the following topics:**

- Registering for QTLS status
- Overseas applications/qualifications
- Recognition route
- Using your workbook
- The review process

# Registering for QTLS status

To apply for Qualified Teacher Learning and Skills (QTLS) status, you will first need to become a member of the Society for Education and Training (SET) by applying and paying a membership fee. SET is recognised by HM Revenue and Customs (HMRC) as a professional body, with membership subscriptions deemed directly relevant to employment. This means that SET members are eligible for tax relief.

You will need to maintain your membership yearly with SET to enable your QTLS status (once achieved) to remain current. As a member of SET you will be able to access professional development opportunities and resources, and communicate with other members.

## Activity

*Before joining SET, take a look at the documents and information at the following links. However, they are quite detailed so you can always read them later if you don't have time now.*

   *SET conditions of membership:* **https://tinyurl.com/yd54eyyd**

   *Membership procedure flowchart:* **https://tinyurl.com/y8xy5d7h**

   *Guidance on suitability for membership:* **https://tinyurl.com/y9q93b8h**

   *Membership procedures: Applications for membership:* **https://tinyurl.com/ycxt62hh**

   *Action against members:* **https://tinyurl.com/y7azwqac**

Being a member of SET shows that you are a professional who is committed to their role, and who will follow all the membership requirements.

There are several different membership grades available, depending upon your current teaching status and your qualifications.

## Activity

*If you are not already a member of SET, go to this page of their website to see the membership grades and prices: https://tinyurl.com/y7mlazkh*

*You can then apply and pay to become a member. If you are unsure of which grade relates to you, further information is available at: https://tinyurl.com/ybdqukkr*

You will need to wait to be accepted as a member of SET before you can apply for QTLS status. Being accepted as a SET member means you must abide by their Code of Professional Practice.

> *The Code of Practice sets out the professional behaviour and conduct expected of members of the Society for Education and Training (SET), including mandatory requirements which must be complied with to become and remain a member. It is a very important statement of what it means to be part of SET, and the levels of professionalism that are required or encouraged of all of our members.*

https://tinyurl.com/y8qavupy (date accessed 16 July 2018)

## Activity

**Take a look at the Code of Professional Practice at this link to make sure you are able to commit to it as part of being a SET member: https://tinyurl.com/m23e9p4**

Once your SET membership has been accepted, you can apply for QTLS status. This is an online process known as *professional formation*. It is completed via SET's website using a program called *My QTLS*.

## Activity

**Before you apply for QTLS status, check if you are eligible via this weblink: https://tinyurl.com/y8apctuy**

There are three *windows* of opportunity each year in which you can register your interest to apply for QTLS status. The dates do not mean you have to start and end within a particular window, just that you can register within them. They are:

- 1 September to 31 October
- 1 December to 31 January
- 1 April to 31 May.

You will need to decide when the best start time (window) will be for you, depending upon your workload. It's important to know that most of the evidence you provide will come from your current practice and research, including being observed with your learners on two occasions. You must be able to commit time and dedication to the process of completing the required activities. This will include meeting with your supporter (covered later), writing statements in an online workbook and uploading evidence of your practice. If you don't feel ready at the moment, you can wait until the next available window to apply.

## Activity

**Check the dates for the current QTLS registration windows (Stage 1) and deadlines (Stage 2) at: https://tinyurl.com/ya5q46ez**

The recommendation for completion is within a four- to six-month period from registration. If you don't make the deadline for completion, SET can defer your application once to the following window of opportunity, at no additional cost. Additional costs will apply if you defer more than once and you will need to start the process again. This is because your evidence must demonstrate your current practice.

### *Tip*

*SET has a comprehensive list of FAQs on their website where you might find answers to any questions you currently have, or might have as you progress through the professional formation process. They can be accessed here: https:// tinyurl.com/ycezx9r3*

## Registration

When you are ready to register for the professional formation process, you will need to be aware that there is a charge which is in addition to your SET membership fee. There are various ways to pay, including by direct debit instalments. A non-refundable deposit will be taken by SET when you apply.

### *Activity*

*Find out how much the professional formation process currently costs, and how to pay, by scrolling down this page: https://tinyurl.com/y9pq9pps*

## Requirements of the professional formation process

To undertake the professional formation process you must have:

- a subject specialism qualification (or a CV which highlights your vocational skills and experience)

- a level 5 or higher initial teacher education (ITE) qualification (you can only submit your workbook once you have been qualified as a teacher for at least six months)

- minimum level 2 qualification in maths and English (or numeracy and literacy). You will need level 3 if you teach these subjects. See the activity on page 16 for examples

- someone who will support you through the process (e.g. a colleague, mentor or manager).

You will need to have access to a scanner or be able to take photo images (in colour) of your original certificates and other evidence (all copies must be clear and legible). You will need to upload the images to your workbook as proof of achievement of your professional qualifications. They must clearly show the dates they were awarded.

## Activity

*Take a look at the following links to see if your maths and English qualifications are listed (and check that you still have your certificates as evidence).*

*Level 2 approved qualifications: https://tinyurl.com/y7jj6a8e*

*Level 3 approved qualifications (for those teaching maths and/or English): https://tinyurl.com/y99q73tx*

It doesn't matter how old your maths and English qualifications are. However, if you do not have any of the stated qualifications it would be beneficial for you to undertake them prior to applying for QTLS status. You may be able to do this via an online course or by attending a taught programme at a reputable training organisation in your local area.

You will need a *supporter* who can observe and comment on your teaching, learning and assessment practice in terms of strengths and areas for development. Ideally, your supporter will be someone you have worked (or are working) closely with who is a more experienced teacher or trainer than you. It would be ideal if they have already achieved QTLS status or at least have a level 5 teaching qualification. Further details of the role of the supporter are explained in Chapter 3.

## Tip

*You might like to think about who your supporter could be, and approach them to check if they are willing and able to take on the role. Further information regarding the role of the supporter can be found at this link: https://tinyurl.com/ybn7rd6s*

## Declaration of suitability

The Society for Education and Training will need to consider your suitability to be a member and, where applicable, to hold QTLS status. Any false declarations will be investigated.

The declaration of suitability form asks you to tick *yes* or *no* to the following questions:

1.  Have you ever been the subject of a bar, partial bar, warning or other action by the Secretary of State or the Disclosure and Barring Service (DBS) in relation to misconduct or working with young people or vulnerable adults?

    Yes   ☐   No   ☐

2.  Have you ever been subject to any disciplinary finding against you by any professional or regulatory body, or by any employer in this country or abroad, or are you currently subject to investigation by such a body or employer?

    Yes   ☐   No   ☐

3a. Have you been convicted of a criminal offence (including motoring offences except fixed penalty notices for speeding and parking fines) or do you have any criminal charges/proceedings pending against you either in this country or abroad? (Note: you should include details of any caution, conditional caution, reprimand, warning, penalty or bind over).

    Yes   ☐   No   ☐

3b. Do you work in a further education institution where the normal duties of that work may involve regular contact with persons aged under 18? (Note: if so, then you must disclose convictions and cautions which are otherwise spent under the Rehabilitation of Offenders Act 1974).

    Yes   ☐   No   ☐

4.  Is there any other information SET should know about which may have a bearing upon your suitability to hold QTLS status or appear on SET's register? (Note: as a registered teacher you will be responsible for upholding and promoting the standards of the profession as set out in SET's Code of Professional Practice. Relevant information would include any involvement in activities which could bring the reputation of the profession into disrepute.)

    Yes   ☐   No   ☐

If you answer yes to any of the questions, you will have the opportunity to add further information during the application process.

## Activity

*Once you are a member of SET, you can access the following page and scroll down until you see* Declaration of Suitability. *Download, print and complete the form. https://tinyurl.com/y7eesmq4*

*Scan the completed form (or take a photo of it) and email it to registrar@et foundation.co.uk using the subject heading of your membership number followed by the letters QTLS. Make sure you use the email address which you used when you registered for the professional formation.*

You will receive an automatic reply to confirm the form has been received. Once you are accepted for the professional formation process, it means you accept and agree to the QTLS terms and conditions.

## Activity

*Take a look at the QTLS terms and conditions at this link: https://tinyurl.com/ ybx3byj6*

If you do not submit your declaration of suitability, your workbook will not be reviewed by SET when you submit it at the end of the professional formation process.

# Overseas applications/qualifications

QTLS status is currently only recognised in England. However, if you are working overseas, you can undertake QTLS status if you are considering working in England, as this might improve your employment prospects.

If you are an overseas applicant (and/or hold an overseas teaching qualification) and you can fulfil the following, you are eligible to apply for QTLS status:

- you teach as part of an English further education (FE) and skills sector provider

- are a member of SET

- you hold the equivalent of a minimum level 5 initial teacher education (ITE) qualification (gained in another country other than England, Wales or Northern Ireland*)

- you hold a minimum level 2 maths qualification**

- you hold a minimum level 2 English qualification**.

*Evidence of authenticity and equivalence for overseas qualifications must be obtained through the National Recognition Information Centre (NARIC) at www.naric.org.uk. NARIC must confirm that your qualification/s entitles you to teach in a secondary school (or above) in the country you are currently in.

**If you teach maths and/or English (such as English as a second language [ESOL] or Functional Skills), your qualifications in these subjects must be at level 3 or higher and also be recognised by NARIC.

## Activity

*If you are an overseas applicant, take a look at the information regarding recognising overseas qualifications here: https://tinyurl.com/yc2kupk6. You can also apply for QTLS via the same page if you wish.*

As an overseas qualified teacher, to undertake the professional formation process, you must be able to evidence that your current teaching practice is underpinned by all 20 of the Professional Standards (as in Appendix 1). This can be demonstrated by mapping your evidence against the standards as you complete your workbook. This is because all English initial teacher education (ITE) qualifications are underpinned by the Professional Standards and an overseas applicant's qualification would not have been.

## Tip

*You can see two different examples of mapping towards the Professional Standards at these links: https://tinyurl.com/ycuq7y6y; https://tinyurl.com/yay d24wl*

SET will review your application to ensure it meets the required standard to obtain QTLS status. This includes a holistic review and moderation of your evidence to ensure that the experience of undertaking the teaching qualification in a country other than England, Wales or Northern Ireland is the equivalent of that taken in the UK, by following a full programme of study to obtain a level 5 ITE qualification. The reviewing panel must be satisfied that the evidence submitted is sufficient. This is to demonstrate full achievement of the learning being claimed, authenticity to prove that the evidence is your own efforts – and is verified as such. It must also be relevant and demonstrate that your current practice is within the FE and skills sector, and not prior learning or experience from elsewhere, such as teaching in a primary school.

# Recognition route

The recognition route is available to practitioners with substantial teaching experience but who do not hold a recognised ITE teaching qualification. It is a process which enables individuals to demonstrate and evidence their practice to the Professional Standards. They will then receive recognition which is equivalent to an initial teacher training qualification at level 5, such as the Diploma in Education and Training (DET).

There are two packages available for SET members who wish to apply for recognition:

- Recognition route only: undertake the recognition route process separately to the professional formation process. If successful, you will receive a certificate of recognition which denotes your experience is equivalent to a level 5 ITE.

- Recognition route combined with QTLS status: undertake both the recognition route and the professional formation process which leads to QTLS status. If you choose this option it will be cheaper than taking both routes separately and only one deposit is required.

## Tip

*SET provides a Technical Guide for members to support them through the recognition route process. You can access a copy at this link: https://tinyurl.com/y7wog8o4*

## Eligibility

Your eligibility to apply for the recognition route will depend upon when your employment as a teacher commenced:

- If your employment commenced before 2007 in the further education (FE) and post 16 skills sector, and you have significant teaching experience of at least five years in the UK before 2007, you are likely to be able to use this route.

- If your employment commenced after 2007, when teaching qualifications were required for all new teachers, you cannot use this route.

You will still need to become a member of SET. Members who successfully complete SET's recognition route will receive a certificate of recognition. This acknowledges the demonstration of their scope, knowledge and practice as being the equivalent of a recognised teaching qualification. It's advisable to check your eligibility with SET prior to applying.

### Activity

*If you feel you are eligible for the recognition route, i.e. you do not hold a recognised teaching qualification (to at least level 5), take a look at this checklist to see what evidence you will need to provide: https://tinyurl.com/y9lpcuuk. You can then apply via this link: https://tinyurl.com/yc8z3sa4*

# Using your workbook

To work towards QTLS status, you will need to use an online workbook, therefore you must have a reliable internet connection. You will be able to add text and upload evidence (also known as *assets*) in support of your professional formation application. SET recommends using a desktop computer with the latest version of Internet Explorer or Chrome as your web browser. Although the systems and technology are compatible with the use of mobiles and tablets, the experience may not be as rewarding.

### Tip

*You will need a computer or a device with a reliable internet connection to be able to complete the professional formation process. You will also need basic computing skills to be able to find your way around your workbook and to upload your evidence – known as* assets.

Assets are pieces of evidence in support of your claim and can include:

- audio files

- electronic documents such as lesson plans and observation reports by your supporter

- images

- photos

- scanned documents such as certificates

- video files.

If you are using evidence which contains your learners' names, you will need to blank these out to keep them confidential.

## Activity

*Take a look at Appendix 2 to view a checklist of the mandatory evidence which is required to achieve QTLS status. This will help you to plan what you need to achieve, and how much time you will need to allocate to generating it. Don't worry if it doesn't make sense at the moment, it will all become clearer as you progress through the process. However, all your evidence (apart from your certificates) must be generated during the professional formation process.*

You might find it useful to use a diary or a calendar to plan some target dates for each aspect of your workbook, and to talk through these with your supporter. You might also like to allocate some time each week where you can work quietly and be undisturbed. As you progress through the professional formation process, you will need plenty of time to complete your workbook, and to undertake continuing professional development (CPD) in relation to the Professional Standards.

## Tip

*SET has produced a timeline to help you with your planning and time management for the professional formation process. A generic link is at the end of the chapter, as it changes for each application window.*

You might like to start getting organised now as this will save you some time as you progress. For example, you could make sure you have the following original certificates accessible:

- initial teacher education (ITE) to at least level 5

- subject specialism (or CV if you don't hold a subject qualification)

- maths

- English.

You could also make sure your CV is up to date as you will need to upload it to your workbook later.

## Tip

*All evidence you use must be from the time you commenced the professional formation process to when you complete. You cannot use anything else (such as an observation which was undertaken when you were working towards an ITE qualification). The only exception is certificates for the following qualifications: teaching; subject specialism; maths and English.*

## Accessing your workbook

Once you have been accepted for the professional formation process, you can use your SET membership number and a password to access your workbook. An email will have been sent to you with this information. If you have not received it, contact SET by calling on 0800 093 9111 or 020 3092 5001.

*My QTLS* is the term used for your workbook; however, it might also be referred to as *PebblePad* or *REfLECT*, and you will also see these terms appearing on your screen.

## Activity

*Once you have been accepted for the professional formation process, take a look at your workbook to familiarise yourself with the content, by following these four steps.*

1. *Access the Society for Education and Training's website at* **https://set.et-foun dation.co.uk / and click on LOG IN, as in Figure 2.1.**

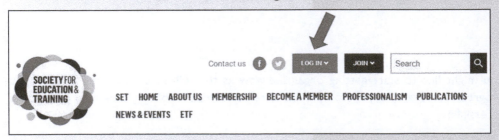

**Figure 2.1 Logging in to SET website**

2.   *You can now enter your details and click on LOGIN, as in Figure 2.2.*

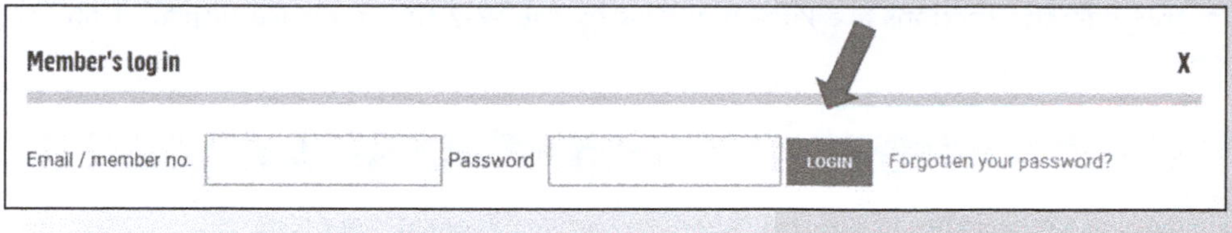

**Figure 2.2  Entering your member details**

3. *You can now click on REfLECT, as in Figure 2.3, to access My QTLS.*

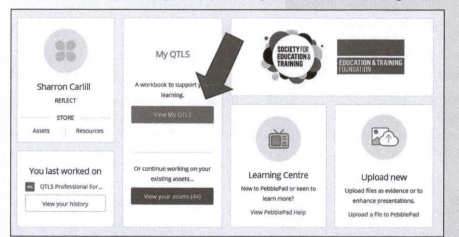

**Figure 2.3  Accessing REfLECT**

*If you have a problem with the next stage, it might be because your internet browser's pop-up blocker or block ads setting is switched on. This will prevent your workbook from opening. The pop-up blocker will be located somewhere in your internet browser settings (these differ for all browsers) and you will need to make sure it is switched off. If you still can't access My QTLS, you might have to delete your browsing history. Again, a way of doing this might be in your browser's settings or you might need to search how to do it as all browsers differ.*

4. *You can now click on View My QTLS to access your workbook, as in Figure 2.4.*

**Figure 2.4  Accessing My QTLS**

*You will now have access to all the sections of your workbook and you will be on the* About You *page to start with.*

## Workbook sections

Once you have accessed your workbook, you will find that various headings are in sections in a grey bar; the sections are known as *tabs* by the way that they are displayed on the screen, as in Figure 2.5.

**Figure 2.5 Workbook sections/tabs**

The following tabs (headings) will be displayed:

- Contents

- About You

- Role and Responsibilities

- Self-Assessment

- Professional Development

- CPD Record

- Critical Reflection

- Final Action Plan

- Sharing Your Workbook

These are all the different sections of the workbook which you will work through during the professional formation process. They can also be accessed by clicking on the *Contents* tab.

There are eight *tabs* or headings in the workbook. Seven of these need to be accessed and completed as you work through the professional formation process. The eighth tab gives information regarding sharing your workbook. These will all be explained in detail throughout the chapters in this book.

---

### Tip

*The* Contents *tab enables you to view all the tabs vertically rather than horizontally. You can then click on the relevant workbook section to access it.*

*The* Save *button enables you to save text and evidence, whereas the* Preview *button allows you to see what you have done without editing your work.*

Don't be afraid to click on any of the icons or buttons on the screen to see what they do. You won't need to use them now, but you may need to as you progress through the professional formation process.

You will need to remember that any information you key into your workbook must be saved, as this does not happen automatically. Make sure you click on the *Save* button as in Figure 2.6 every time you have completed something. However, if you have not saved for a while, a prompt will appear on the screen to remind you.

**Figure 2.6  Saving your work**

You might find it useful to copy and paste your text independently from your workbook, for example to a word processed document. This would enable you to save it elsewhere (i.e. if you don't have an internet connection) or in case you forget to save it to your workbook.

## Activity

*Take a look at all of the sections of your workbook to familiarise yourself with them, and what is required during the professional formation process. Don't be too concerned if it doesn't make sense, it will become clearer as you progress.*

*Logging out*

When you are ready to log out, click on the ⬛ icon in the top right-hand corner of your screen. When you use this icon, a prompt will appear to enable you to save your work. Closing your browser does not log you out and will give access to others if you share your computer.

## Using an alternative format for the professional formation process

It is an expectation that you use the workbook. However, in exceptional circumstances, you can apply to use an alternative format route. This route is only available for applicants who have a disability or illness, or who are unable to access technology, perhaps due to working in a secure environment such as a prison. If this applies to you and you are accepted, you will be able to continue with your application via a paper-based workbook.

**Activity**

*If you are eligible and wish to apply to use an alternative format for your professional formation process, contact SET directly to discuss your requirements on telephone number 0800 093 9111 or email them at membership.enquiries@ etfoundation.co.uk*

# The review process

You might be wondering how SET makes the decision to confer QTLS status once you have completed your workbook. All applications for the professional formation process must be *reviewed* before QTLS status can be awarded. The process is based on reviewing the content of your workbook, as well as your CPD and your reflections. It is conducted by a team of SET trained reviewers and moderators.

Following the review of your workbook, SET and its moderators will make a decision as to whether your application has been *successful*, or *has not sufficiently met the criteria*.

## Successful

Your workbook will be reviewed the month following the official submission date. You will be notified of your result within eight weeks of this date.

You will be able to access your reviewer's feedback and an electronic QTLS certificate via your workbook. You will also receive a hard copy of your certificate in the post around six to eight weeks after receiving your result.

## Has not sufficiently met the criteria

If you haven't met the criteria, you will receive an email stating this, and you will be able to view constructive and developmental feedback from your reviewer via your workbook.

If you just need to add a bit more text and/or evidence, you can reapply at any time, but preferably within six weeks of receiving your result. SET can normally turn around reapplications within two weeks of receiving them, so you don't need to wait until the next review period, and there is currently no charge.

If you have any questions regarding your resubmission, staff at SET will be happy to advise you.

If you disagree with your reviewer's decision, you can appeal and you will be informed of the process to follow by SET.

*What are the review criteria?*

The workbook needs to contain sufficient information for judgements to be made. It needs to be approved as being all your own work, which should be relevant to both the review criteria and your job role.

Reviewers are asked to examine the evidence and evaluate whether the criteria have been met by the following:

- Sufficiency: does the application contain the required evidence for standardised and personalised elements?

- Authenticity: does the application clearly relate to the member who has submitted it?

- Relevance: is the application relevant to the member's work?

Statistics (at the time of publication) show that the achievement rate of those successfully completing QTLS status is over 85 per cent.

### Tip

*There is lots of helpful guidance, templates and videos at this link, which you might find useful to access as you progress through the professional formation process:* https://tinyurl.com/SETGuidance

## What makes a good application for QTLS status?

You could consider the following points when working through the application process; they won't make sense at the moment, but they will as you progress through the book.

- Devising a strong self-assessment, marking the beginning of your journey.

- Having a thread running through the whole process, with everything relating back to your self-assessment and professional development plan.

- Being selective and focused with regards to your CPD, i.e. not trying to do too much.

- Writing a clear and precise narrative with quality evidence added at each stage of the process.

- Writing a strong critical reflection of the impact of the journey on your practice, your learners and the organisation.

- Providing evidence that your learners have clearly benefited.

- Referencing to relevant educational theory and research.

- Having an active supporter throughout the process who provides a strong supporting statement, confirming your progression and development.

You might wish to return to this bullet list as you progress through the professional formation process.

# Summary

This chapter has explored how to become a member of the Society for Education and Training (SET), how to apply for the professional formation process, how to use your workbook, and what happens when you have completed it.

You might like to carry out further research by accessing the books and websites listed at the end of this chapter.

This chapter has covered the following topics:

- Registering for QTLS status
- Overseas applications/qualifications
- Recognition route
- Using your workbook
- The review process

# References and further information

Castle, P. and Buckler, S. (2009) *How to be a Successful Teacher*. London: SAGE.

Clark, R. C. (2015) *Evidence-Based Training Methods: A Guide for Training Professionals* (2nd edition). ATD Press.

Gravells, A. (2015) *Principles and Practices of Assessment*. London: SAGE/Learning Matters.

Gravells, A. (2016) *Principles and Practices of Quality Assurance*. London: SAGE/Learning Matters.

Gravells, A. (2017) *Principles and Practices of Teaching and Training*. London: SAGE/Learning Matters.

Petty, G. (2009) *Evidence-based Teaching: A Practical Approach* (2nd edition). Cheltenham: Nelson Thornes.

Tummons, J. (2010) *Becoming a Professional Tutor* (2nd edition). Exeter: Learning Matters.

# Websites

Education and Training Foundation (ETF) – www.et-foundation.co.uk

National Recognition Information Centre (NARIC) – www.naric.org.uk.

Professional Standards for Teachers and Trainers – https://tinyurl.com/o2cv9fs

QTLS timeline (under the *My QTLS* heading) – https://tinyurl.com/y7eesmq4

Society for Education and Training (SET) – https://set.et-foundation.co.uk

# 3

# About you

**Introduction**

This chapter will assist you in completing the first stage of your workbook by asking you to work through various activities.

It will explain how to input information about yourself, your professional background, and how to upload copies of your certificates to your workbook.

It will also guide you about the role of your supporter, and how to track your progress.

**This chapter will cover the following topics:**

- About you
- Qualifications
- Your supporter
- Progress tracking

# About you

The *About You* section of the workbook is the beginning of the professional formation process. It starts with a confirmation of your personal details, which you will need to check online first.

## Activity

*Access your workbook as before (as in Chapter 2) and go to the About You section by clicking on the About You tab.*

Once you have accessed your workbook, you will see the different sections across the top of the screen. These are known as *tabs* and the first one is *About You*, as in Figure 3.1.

**Figure 3.1 Accessing the About You tab and checking your details**

## Activity

*Once you have clicked on the About You tab, your name, member number and other details will already be on the page. Check the spelling and order of your first and last name. This is how it will appear on your certificate once you have achieved QTLS status. Check that your Declaration of suitability is marked as received. You will have completed the declaration as part of your original application (as explained in Chapter 2). Contact the Society for Education and Training (SET) by emailing registrar@etfoundation.co.uk if the declaration of suitability is marked as has not yet been received. Include your membership number when contacting them.*

If your declaration of suitability is not received by SET, your workbook will not be reviewed when you submit it at the end of the professional formation process.

## Period of professional formation

In this section of the *About You* page, you are required to input some dates. During the professional formation process, you must demonstrate your professional development over a minimum period of four to six months.

You will need to set realistic and achievable dates which suit you, your learners and your organisation's needs. If you are not successful, you can resubmit your application, see Chapter 2 for details.

### Activity

*Click on the calendar icon in* From, *as in Figure 3.2 and add the date you registered for QTLS status. Click on the calendar icon in* To *and add the proposed date you will complete and submit your workbook to SET. Your registration and submission (application) must be within the* Stage 1 *and* Stage 2 *dates as shown on this page:* **https://tinyurl.com/ya5q46ez**

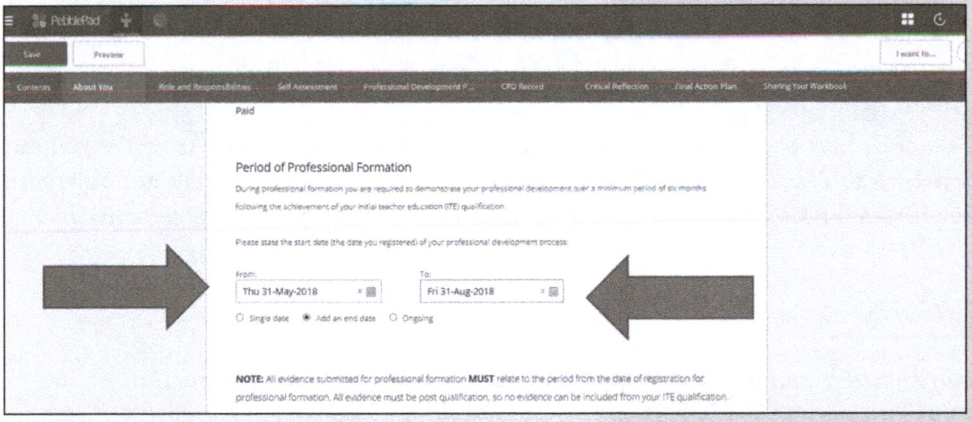

**Figure 3.2 Inputting the dates of your professional formation**

### Tip

*Save your workbook regularly. Use the* Save *button at the top left of the screen, as in Figure 2.6 in Chapter 2. At this point, DO NOT click on the* Share with Supporter *button in the bottom right corner (as you won't be able to add anything else to your workbook). However, if you do click the button in error, there is an option to click the* unshare *button which resets your workbook to edit mode and you won't lose anything.*

When you first save anything, you will receive a message that you have auto-submitted your workbook to a workspace. This is the correct process and ensures your workbook will be allocated to the correct review period when complete. It does not mean that you have shared your workbook with SET (which is the final part of the professional formation process).

# Qualifications

In this section of the *About You* page you will need to upload clear full colour copies of your original certificates, and enter relevant dates of achievement. You can scan or take a digital photo of them.

## Tip

*You will find it will save time as you progress through this section of your workbook if you have your original qualifications and documents accessible, i.e.:*

- *teaching qualification (supported by NARIC statements and mapping evidence if gained overseas – see Chapter 2)*
- *subject specialism qualification (or CV and job description)*
- *maths qualification (and any recent updates if relevant)*
- *English qualification (and any recent updates if relevant).*

If you don't have original versions of the above, or are waiting for them to arrive, you can come back to this section later. You must have achieved the required certificates otherwise your application for QTLS status will be reviewed as *has not sufficiently met the criteria.*

## Activity

*Read the text under the heading* Qualifications *in the relevant section of the* About You *part of the workbook. There are links to further information if you need to check anything.*

## Initial teacher education qualification

You must have achieved an initial teacher education (ITE) qualification (to at least level 5), and have been qualified for at least six months. This must have included at least 100 hours of teaching practice and eight observed lessons.

Examples are:

- Level 5 Diploma in Education and Training (DET)
- Level 5 Certificate in Education (CertEd)

- Level 6 Professional Graduate Certificate in Education

- Level 7 Post Graduate Certificate in Education (PGCE).

## Tip

*You can see a full list of equivalent ITE qualifications at this link: https://tinyurl.com/y9ckq754*

*If you are unsure if your qualification meets the requirements, you can email*

*membership.enquiries@etfoundation.co.uk*

Teachers working in schools are eligible to apply for QTLS status. However, if this applies to you, you will be required to evidence that you are currently teaching learners aged 14 plus (i.e. in years 10, 11 and above) and/or with adults. This is to enable you to demonstrate you are developing knowledge and skills relevant to the further education and skills sector (as this sector relates to QTLS status). If you have an overseas ITE qualification, you are also eligible to apply. As part of your application you will need to provide a statement from the UK National Recognition Information Centre (NARIC) which confirms that your teaching qualification is equivalent to level 5, and entitles you to teach in a secondary school (or above) in the country you are currently in (see Chapter 2). In addition, you will be required to provide additional evidence as part of your workbook.

## Activity

*Add the date you started working towards your ITE qualification and the date you achieved it, by clicking on the date areas, as in Figure 3.3. If you achieved the qualification by sitting an exam and did not attend classes, there is an option to click on* Single date *to input the date of certification.*

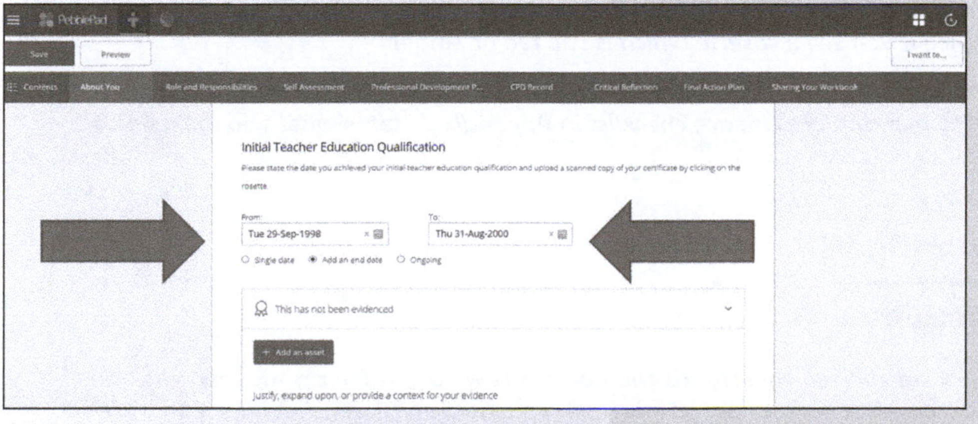

**Figure 3.3 Adding the dates of your ITE qualifications**

If you are still completing your qualification, you can click on *ongoing*. However, you must have been qualified for at least six months before submitting your final workbook. You will need to remember to return to this page and upload a copy of your certificate once you receive it.

## Activity

*If you haven't already done so, take a scan or a photo of your teaching qualification certificate. Make sure the image is clear and in colour. Save it to your device with a relevant filename, and in a place you can access it later for uploading to your workbook.*

*Uploading your certificates*

Under each qualification heading, after the date, you will see a red rosette icon with a down arrow (v symbol) to the right. You can either click on the rosette or the v symbol to upload your supporting evidence, as in Figure 3.4. Your evidence must be a clearly scanned colour copy or photo image of your certificate.

**Figure 3.4  Uploading evidence**

## Tip

*Throughout your workbook, the rosettes will change colour from red to amber (to denote some more evidence is required) and then to green (to denote the section is fully evidenced). You can go back to any section later to add more evidence if you see a rosette which is still red or amber.*

*It's not mandatory to upload evidence to every rosette in the workbook. The QTLS mandatory evidence checklist in Appendix 2 states what you must upload.*

## Activity

*Click on the red rosette (or the down arrow to the far right), then click on the Add an asset button, as in Figure 3.5 (an asset is a piece of evidence you are submitting by uploading it). Then click on UPLOAD. Before or after uploading, you can add a few notes in the text box to justify your evidence.*

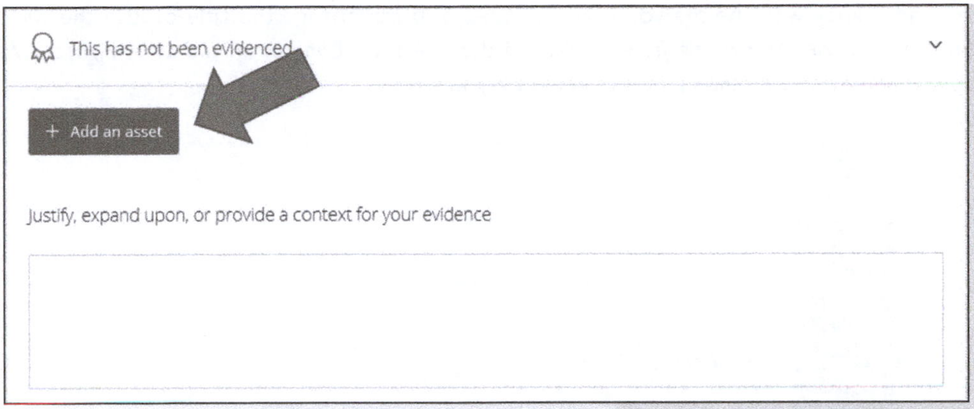

This has not been evidenced

+ Add an asset

Justify, expand upon, or provide a context for your evidence

**Figure 3.5  Adding an asset**

*The process to upload an asset (evidence) is the same in all the sections of the workbook. Once you have uploaded an asset, you have the option to add an additional asset if you wish. Each time you upload an asset, you have the option to justify it by keying in text in the box on the screen.*

There are two options for completing the upload process, as in Figure 3.6. The first (arrow 1) is to *drag and drop* the relevant file or image into the *Drag a file here* box (locate the file or image on your device first, then click on it and hold your click whilst dragging it over, then release). The second (arrow 2) is to click on the *Or choose a file* box. If you choose a file, you will be able to locate it from your device to upload it.

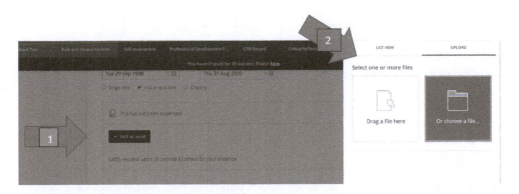

**Figure 3.6  Choosing a file to upload**

The option you choose will depend on your computer or the device you are using. You will then be able to *Change file* or *Remove*, as in Figure 3.7.

If you are happy with the file you have uploaded, you can change the title of it in the section called *Please enter a title for your file*, and then click on *Confirm upload* as in Figure 3.7. You can add more evidence in the same way if you wish.

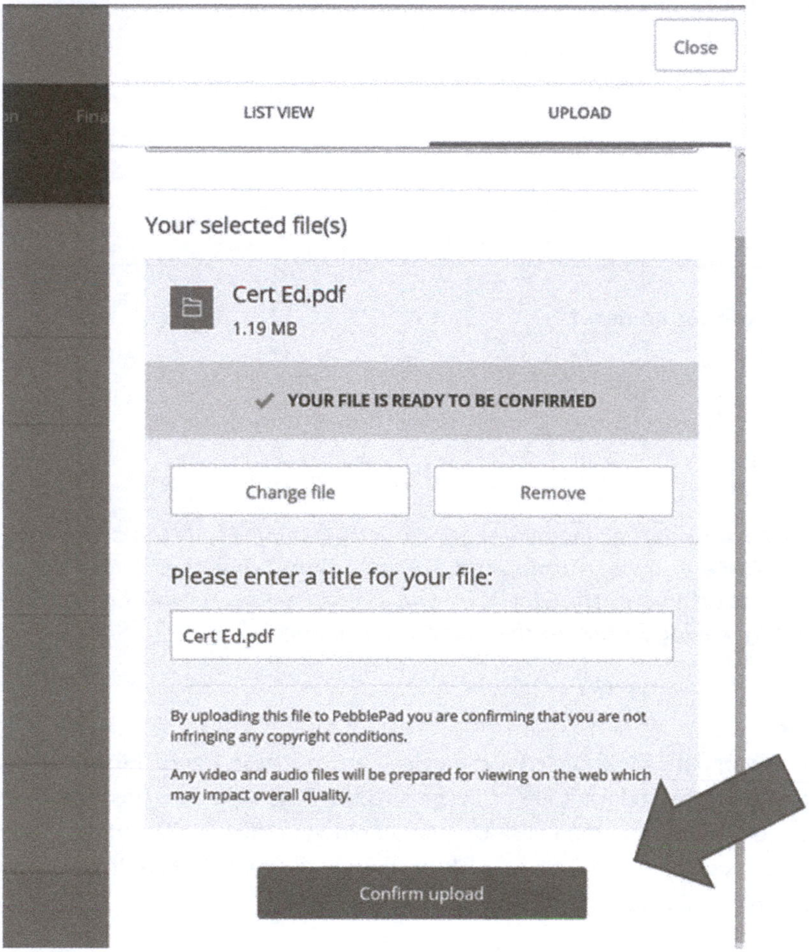

**Figure 3.7  Uploading evidence**

Once you have uploaded your evidence, you will notice the red rosette has changed colour. If it's amber, it means you still have more evidence to upload in a section.

**Tip**

*If you wish to use a piece of evidence which you have previously uploaded, perhaps in another section of your workbook, just click on* **LIST VIEW** *instead of* **UPLOAD** *(at the top of Figure 3.7). All your files will be listed and you can click on the one you want, followed by* **Done** *at the bottom of the window.*

You can add comments to the box which is headed *Justify, expand upon, or provide a context for your evidence*. This could be a comment which states the title of your qualification.

Below the box, you will see the question *To what extent does this evidence prove what you can do or have done?*

You can then click in a relevant circle to make your choice:

- This item has not yet been evidenced

- This item is not yet fully evidenced

- This item is now fully evidenced

You will find that this statement appears regularly throughout your workbook. Make sure you click on the relevant option. It acts as a reminder as the first option keeps the rosette red, the second changes it to amber and the third changes it to green.

## Activity

*Upload your evidence and key in a title name for your file, for example, ITE Certificate or Cert Ed and click Confirm upload as in Figure 3.7. The rosette will change to an amber colour and will not turn green until you click on this item is now fully evidenced located at the bottom of the workbook section.*

It is not mandatory to upload evidence to every rosette within the workbook. However, you must upload all of the mandatory evidence, as in Appendix 2, as you progress through the professional formation process. When you upload evidence, a message will state how many *linked assets* you have uploaded, as in Figure 3.8. A linked asset means you have linked a piece of evidence (a document, image, digital, audio or visual clip) to a section of your workbook.

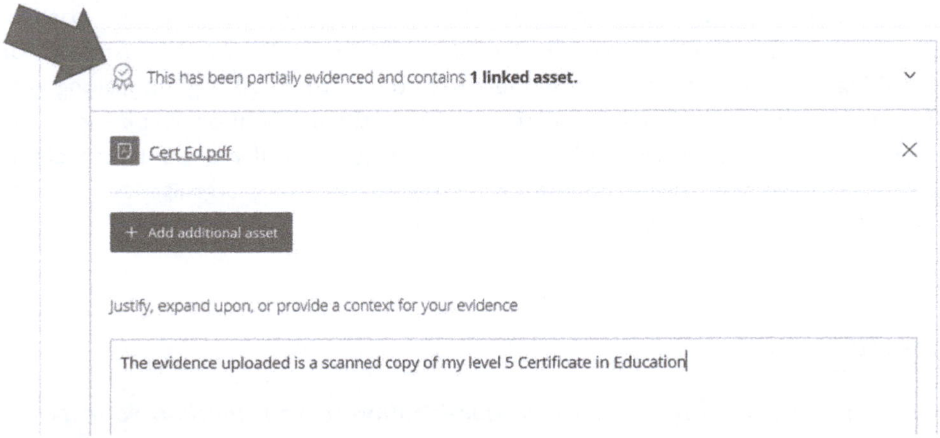

**Figure 3.8 Uploading your ITE qualifications**

## Subject specialist qualification

If you hold a subject specialist qualification, i.e. you are qualified in the same subject you are currently teaching, you will need to upload a copy of your certificate in this section of your workbook. If you don't, you will need to upload your CV instead. You can also add your job description which highlights your role and responsibilities.

**Tip**

*Make sure your CV is up to date, even if you don't need to upload it at this time, you will need it for the next section of your workbook. You could search the internet for guidance regarding compiling a CV if you are not sure how to create one.*

As you will be an experienced practitioner in your *subject*, and also a professional *teacher*, the term *dual professional* is often used to denote your role. This is because you are a professional in two different aspects. The subject you teach might not require you to hold a specific subject specialist qualification at all, but just possess the necessary skills, knowledge and experience. If you are teaching towards an accredited qualification, you will need to find out what the requirements for you to teach it might be. There is often a particular body responsible for your subject. In the UK, it's the Federation for Industry Sector Skills and Standards and you can access their website at: http://fisss.org. They, along with the awarding organisation who accredit and certificate the qualification, will decide what is required by teachers to deliver and assess in each subject area. If you are unsure, obtain a copy of the qualification specification from the relevant awarding organisation's website and take a look at it to see what the requirements are.

**Activity**

*Add the date of your subject specialist qualification to your workbook, in the same way as before.*

*Take a scan or a photo (in colour) of your subject specialist qualification certificate. Make sure the image is clear and save it to your device. You will now be able to upload one or more images, just like before. If you don't have a certificate, make sure your CV is up to date and upload it instead. You can add text to the box if you wish, and then choose This item is now fully evidenced.*

Once you have uploaded a copy of your certificate or CV, you will be able to save it as before, and a green rosette will confirm you have linked an asset to this section of your workbook.

## Level 2 maths qualification

To achieve QTLS status, you must hold at least a level 2 qualification in maths or its equivalent. Although the heading in the workbook states *Level 2*, it's fine to hold a higher level.

Your maths qualification must be on the list of acceptable qualifications. There is a link in this section of your workbook to access the current list. If you teach maths as your subject specialism, for example, you are a maths Functional Skills tutor or maths GCSE tutor, you will be required to demonstrate you are qualified at level 3 or above.

## Activity

*Take a look at the list of acceptable level 2 maths qualifications at this link: https://tinyurl.com/y7jj6a8e*

*Level 3 are at this link: https://tinyurl.com/y99q73tx*

It is good practice (but not mandatory) to update your skills if they are five years or older. This will demonstrate that your knowledge and skills are current. You might like to undertake some free online modules which are offered by the Education and Training Foundation's online learning programme at https://tinyurl.com/y9zl9nle

## Activity

*Add the date of your maths qualification to your workbook. Take a scan or a photo (in colour) of your maths qualification certificate. Make sure the image is clear and save it to your device. You will now be able to upload it to your workbook, along with any supporting evidence of updates. You can add text to the box if you wish, and then choose This item is now fully evidenced.*

Once you have uploaded a copy of your certificate, you will be able to save it as before, and a green rosette will confirm you have linked an asset to this section of your workbook. You will have the opportunity to add an additional asset if you wish (as in Figure 3.9) and to make comments about your evidence.

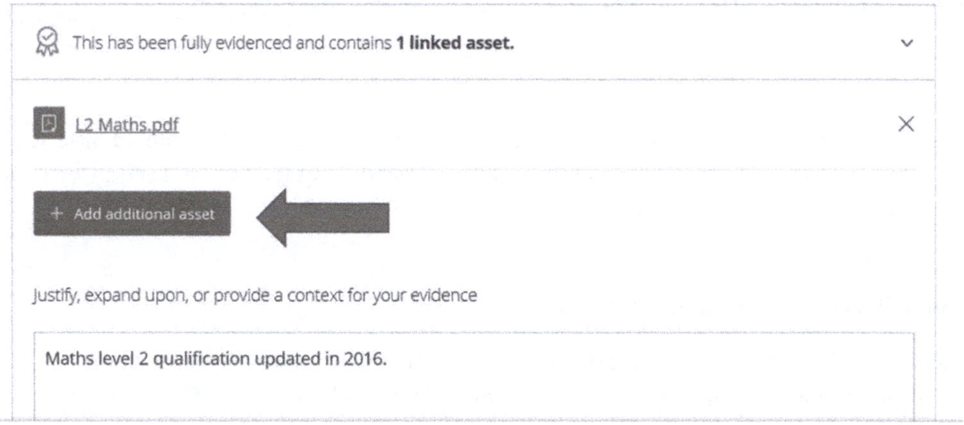

**Figure 3.9  Evidencing your maths qualification**

## Level 2 English qualification

To achieve QTLS status, you must hold at least a level 2 qualification in English or its equivalent, for example, literacy. Although the heading in the workbook states *Level 2* it's fine to hold a higher level.

Your English qualification must be on the list of acceptable qualifications. There is also a link in this section of your workbook to access the current list. If you teach English as your subject specialism, for example, as an English Functional Skills, GCSE tutor or English for Speakers of Other Languages (ESOL) tutor, you will be required to demonstrate you are qualified at level 3 or above.

### *Activity*

*Take a look at the list of acceptable level 2 English qualifications at this link: https://tinyurl.com/y7jj6a8e*

*Level 3 are at this link: https://tinyurl.com/y99q73tx*

### *Activity*

*Add the date of your English qualification to your workbook. Take a scan or a photo (in colour) of your English qualification certificate. Make sure the image is*

*clear and save it to your device. You will now be able to upload it to your work-*
*book, along with any supporting evidence of updates. You can add text to the*
*box if you wish, and then choose* This item is now fully evidenced.

Once you have uploaded a copy of your certificate, you will be able to save it as before, and a green rosette will confirm you have linked an asset to this section of your workbook. You will have the opportunity to add an additional asset if you wish and to make comments about your evidence.

## Tip

*The preferred formats for scanned documents, images and photographs are jpeg*
*or pdf. However, you may be able to upload other formats such as:*

*.avi, .bmp, .doc, .docx, .gif, .jpg, .pdf, .pps, .ppt, .pub, .rtf, .tif, .txt, .xls, .xlsx and*
*.zip.*

# Your supporter

Your supporter will ideally already have QTLS status or at least be qualified to level 5 ITE, be a more experienced teacher than you and be a member of SET. However, SET does recognise this may not always be possible and will consider a supporter if they have:

- known you in a professional capacity for a minimum of six months (but not a friend, family member, or be undertaking QTLS themselves)

- have a wide-ranging experience of the sector

- have knowledge of a relevant subject specialist area or teaching practice

- can give an accurate testimonial regarding your current practice.

## Activity

*Read the text under the heading* Your Supporter *in the relevant section of the*
About You *part of the workbook.*

Your supporter should have experience of passing judgements regarding teaching, learning and assessment. For example, they are in a position to carry out and document obser-vations of your teaching, learning and assessment practice. They must be able to provide constructive feedback to support your professional development. They could be your mentor or manager.

*Your supporter should be someone you trust, and feel you can openly speak to. You should ask them if they are willing to take on the role before adding their name to your workbook.*

The supporter's role is to work closely with you from the beginning of the professional formation process, and to provide ongoing guidance, support and feedback as you progress through your workbook. Their role is key to helping you develop your professional values, attributes, knowledge, understanding and professional skills, as in the Professional Standards (see Appendix 1).

It is possible for your supporter to undertake an *Introduction to Mentoring* programme (currently free). There is a module specifically for QTLS supporters and they don't need to be a member of SET to undertake it. More details can be found here: https://tinyurl.com/ya5zjybj

As well as formal observations of your teaching, learning and assessment practice, your supporter will hold professional discussions with you and document them. They will complete the template provided by SET which you can then upload to your workbook as further evidence of your professional practice.

*Take a look at this page of SET's website for more information regarding the role of the supporter and the template they will use: https://tinyurl.com/ybn7rd6s*

You might like to ask your supporter to look at the information at the above link and familiarise themselves with the template they will need to complete. It would be useful to agree some dates to meet with them, which fit in with the various dates you have set yourself to complete your workbook.

**Activity**

*Complete the* Your Supporter *section with the relevant information, as in* Figure 3.10. *You will need to input their first and last name. If they have not been added to the system before, you will be prompted to add them.*

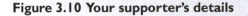

> **Your Supporter**
>
> Your supporter will be a qualified teacher acting as your critical friend or mentor and will be able to provide feedback throughout the process. More guidance on the role of the supporter can be found here. Enter the first and last name of your supporter. If you have not used this person's name previously, additional boxes will appear which will ask you to give the person's name and email address.
>
> | Vlad Ivanovs | White Rose School | × |
> | vlad@ | Education Manager | |

**Figure 3.10 Your supporter's details**

---

**Tip**

*If you haven't saved your work for 30 minutes, a prompt will appear on the screen to remind you.*

---

## Evidence from your supporter

Your supporter will need to provide evidence in support of your professional formation. The mandatory requirements are:

- one professional discussion (using a template provided by SET)

- two observations with at least three months between them (however, your supporter might not carry out the observations, for example, your manager or mentor could do them). The observation report will be on your organisation's own template

- one supporting statement (responding to a series of questions by SET). This will be after you have shared your workbook with them at the end of the professional formation process.

*Professional discussion*

A professional discussion is a conversation with your supporter, rather than questions and answers. It gives you the opportunity to justify what you have achieved, and to gain advice and support. Having a professional discussion is a good way to demonstrate your progress, particularly if you have difficulty expressing yourself in writing. Think of the professional discussion as an opportunity to clarify any issues and to discuss how you feel you are progressing.

---

**Tip**

*Remember to refer to the Professional Standards (see Appendix 1), and describe how you are meeting them, when undertaking your professional discussion with your supporter.*

SET guidance suggests three professional discussions (although only one is mandatory) between yourself and your supporter. For example, you may wish to share and discuss your professional development plan (PDP) with them once you have completed the self-assessment process (as in Chapters 5 and 6). This could include how you have met any action points as a result of your first observation, and would be in addition to the mandatory professional discussion.

The mandatory professional discussion (known as the *interim* discussion) is based on your progress towards your continuing professional development (CPD) record and will be explained in Chapter 7. A final optional professional discussion could be to discuss the impact of your development and to identify details of further professional development in your final action plan, explained in Chapter 9.

## Observations

You will be formally observed by your supporter on at least two occasions throughout the time you are working towards QTLS status. However, you can ask your supporter to observe you more if you wish.

The first observation must be undertaken within one month of the date you registered for the professional formation process. The second observation should not take place until three months after the first, and be no more than one month before submitting your completed workbook.

Your observed practice must be demonstrated with learners aged 14 plus (i.e. in years 10, 11 and above) and/or with adults.

If you miss the one-month deadline for your first observation, you must make sure your final observation is at least three months afterwards, and before the deadline for submitting your workbook to SET.

The observations can be by your supporter and/or someone you work closely with, such as your manager or a mentor. They will need to use the observation form which is normally used within your organisation as one is not supplied by SET. The observation can help to identify areas which will inform your professional development plan (PDP), which is covered in Chapter 6.

## Tip

*You might like to think about contacting your observer now to agree the dates and times they will observe you. Remember that you need two observations which are three months apart. The first must be within one month of commencing, and the second should be no more than one month before submitting your completed workbook.*

## Supporting statement

The final mandatory role your supporter will undertake is completing the *supporting statement*. The supporting statement consists of a series of questions, which might take about an hour to complete. However, it might take your supporter much longer to read your text in your workbook and review your evidence. Details regarding the supporting statement will be explained further in Chapter 9.

## Tip

*Agree a date well in advance with your supporter as to when you will be sharing your final workbook with them. This should be approximately two weeks prior to your submission deadline. This will help them to plan some time to review your workbook and respond to the questions from SET.*

You will need to share your workbook with your supporter two weeks prior to the deadline for submitting your workbook to SET. Prior to sharing your workbook with your supporter, you should proof read all of your work carefully. This is to check for spelling and grammatical errors, and that you have completed everything you should have. You might like to ask a colleague or a friend to read it too, as they might see some typing errors which you have not noticed. Once you formally share your workbook with your supporter at the end of the professional formation process, you can no longer add or edit any of your work.

*Sharing pages of your workbook with others*

You can informally share pages of your workbook at any time with your supporter, a friend, a colleague or another QTLS applicant. This would be a valuable way to gain ongoing feedback. It is via the *I want to....* button at the top right of the screen, as in Figure 3.11. It will not prevent you from adding or editing your work if you do it this way.

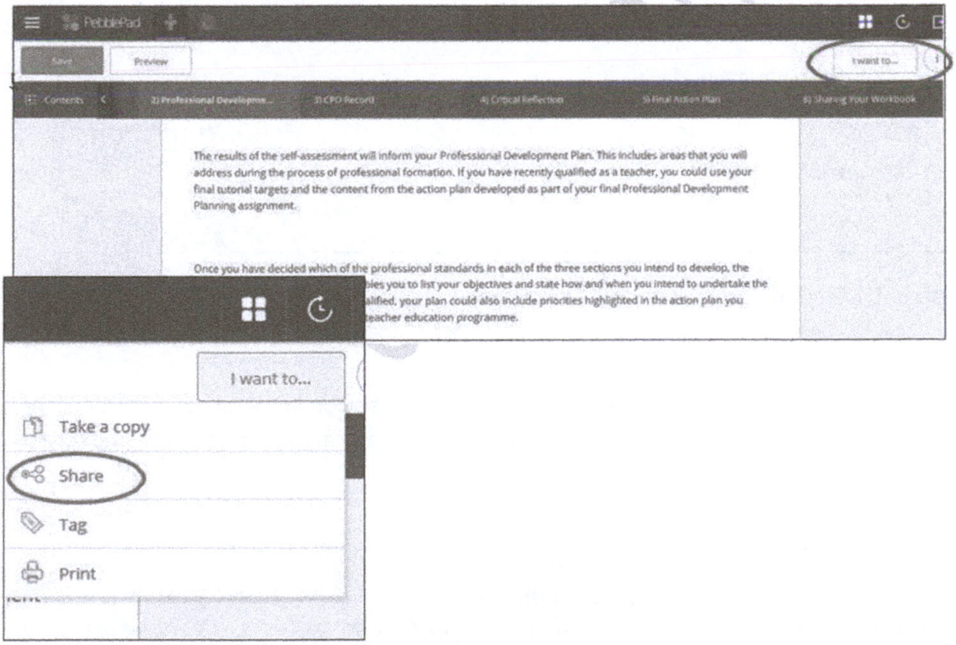

**Figure 3.11  Sharing pages of your workbook**

## Activity

*Click on the* I want to… *button, as in* Figure 3.11, *then click on* Share, *scroll down and choose* With people (known as recipients). *Key in the person's name, if they have not been added to the system before you will be prompted to add them. You can then choose what you would like them to see, add a comment and click on* Share asset.

They will receive an email and be able to access your workbook to give you feedback. You will be able to view the feedback by clicking on the ⓘ symbol in the top right-hand corner of your screen and then clicking on the word *FEEDBACK*.

# Progress tracking

Once you have completed all the sections in the *About You* page of your workbook, you can mark it as complete. This helps you to track your progress throughout the professional formation process.

## Activity

*Tick the box at the end of the page to* Mark page as complete, *as in Figure 3.12 (once you are sure it is all completed).*

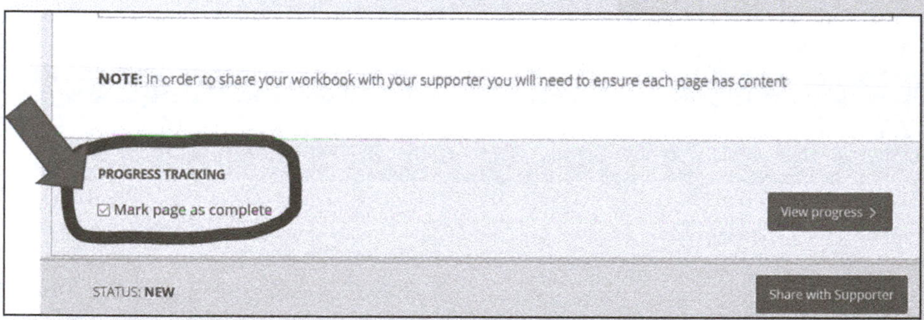

**NOTE:** In order to share your workbook with your supporter you will need to ensure each page has content

**PROGRESS TRACKING**
☑ Mark page as complete

View progress >

STATUS: **NEW**

Share with Supporter

**Figure 3.12 Marking the page as complete**

At this point, DO NOT click on the *Share with supporter* button in the bottom right corner of the page. There will be the opportunity to do this when you have completed your workbook.

## Tip

*If you want to go back to a page later to add something to it, don't mark it as complete. For example, if you need to upload a copy of a certificate which you have not yet received.*

# Viewing your progress

To help you keep track of your progress throughout the professional formation process, you can click on the *View progress* link at the bottom right of any workbook page, as in Figure 3.12. A new window will open, if you click on the *PROGRESS* tab, as in Figure 3.13; you can see which sections of the workbook you have:

- completed (in green text)

- are in progress (in amber text)

- have not started (in red text).

You can also see, as a percentage, how far you are through the professional formation process.

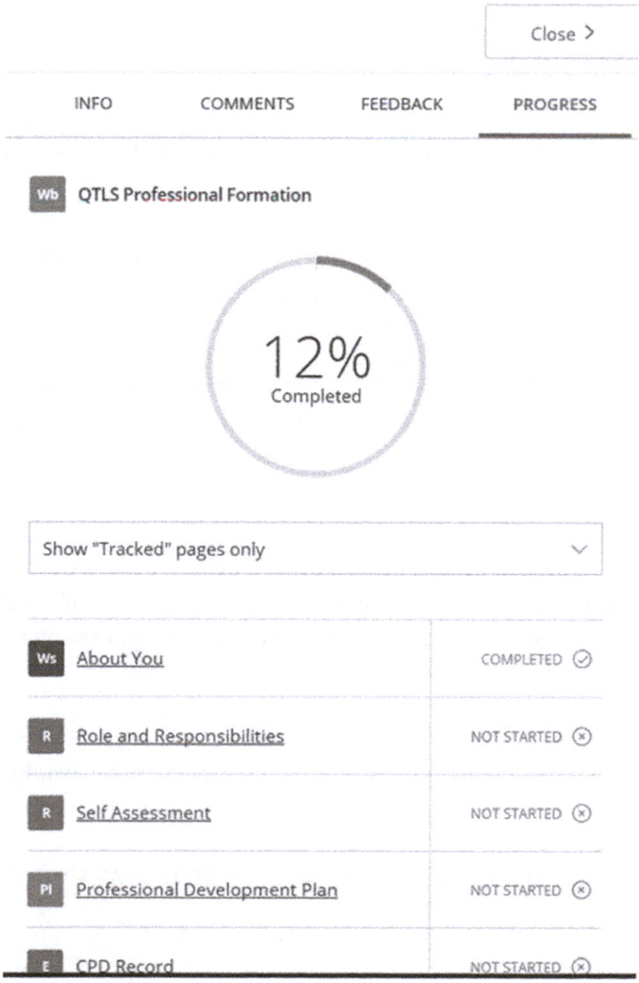

**Figure 3.13 Viewing your progress**

There are four headings in this new window:

- INFO – gives you basic information, for example, the last time you modified your workbook

- COMMENTS – enables you to add comments to your assets (evidence), you can also do this within the workbook page

- FEEDBACK – enables you to view any feedback from people you have shared your workbook with

- PROGRESS – enables you to track your progress.

You can click on *Close* to clear it from your screen.

Sometimes, this icon will appear on your screen: ; clicking on it will take you to the window as shown in Figure 3.13.

## Other icons on your screen

You may have noticed that there are other icons on your screen. You don't need to use them if you don't want to, and they might even confuse you at the moment. However, this is what they do:

☰ Click on this icon as a short cut to your *Asset store* (all the evidence you have uploaded so far), and to the *Resource store*. There are also some other options if you wish to use them. Click the same icon again to close the window. If you use the back button on your browser you will need to click on *View My QTLS* to get back into the workbook.

▪ PebblePad Click on this icon to take you back to the View My QTLS page. PebblePad is the software platform used for your workbook.

⬆ Works in the same way as the above icon.

◑ Click on this icon to view your dashboard, which opens in a new window. You will need to close the window to get back to your workbook. Don't worry about what appears on the screen as it won't affect you at the moment.

⊞ Click on this icon to search your workbook. If you have uploaded assets (evidence), you will be able to click on anything listed to view it. You will need to click outside this window to return to your workbook.

↻ Click on this icon to view what you have been working on. Click on *Close* to clear the window.

▣ Click on this icon to log out. Click cancel if you don't want to. If you choose to log out, a new window will appear. If you have logged out in error, you can just log back in again by clicking on *Login to PebblePad*.

### Activity

*If you have time, click on the different icons to see what happens and where they take you. However, don't worry too much about them as you can choose not to use them if you wish.*

# Summary

This chapter has explored how to complete the first stage of your workbook. This included inputting information about yourself, your professional background and uploading copies of your certificates to your workbook. It also introduced you to the role of your supporter, and how to track your progress.

You might like to carry out further research by accessing the books and websites listed at the end of this chapter.

This chapter has covered the following topics:

- About you
- Qualifications
- Your supporter
- Progress tracking

# References and further information

Allan, D. (2017) *Teaching English and Maths in FE*. London: SAGE/Learning Matters.

CGP (2016) *Functional Skills English*. Broughton in Furness: Coordination Group.

CGP (2016) *Functional Skills ICT*. Broughton in Furness: Coordination Group.

CGP (2016) *Functional Skills Maths*. Broughton in Furness: Coordination Group.

Hughes, N. (2010) *Teaching Adult Literacy*. Oxford: OU Press.

Paton, A. (2009) *Teaching Adult ESOL*. Oxford: OU Press.

White, J. (2015) *Digital Literacy Skills for FE Teachers*. London: SAGE/Learning Matters.

Wyse, D., Jones, R., Bradford, H. and Wolpert, M.A. (2018) *Teaching English, Language and Literacy* (3rd edition). London: Routledge.

# Websites

Education and Training Foundation (ETF) – www.et-foundation.co.uk

Professional Standards for Teachers and Trainers – https://tinyurl.com/o2cv9fs

Supporting Practitioners in Maths and English – https://tinyurl.com/y84n2uyf

Federation for Industry Sector Skills and Standards – http://fisss.org

National Recognition Information Centre – www.naric.org.uk

Society for Education and Training (SET) – https://set.et-foundation.co.uk

# 4

# Role and responsibilities

## Introduction

This chapter will assist you in completing the second stage of your workbook by asking you to work through various activities.

It will explain how to input information to your workbook regarding your role and responsibilities, your teaching career and your motivation for undertaking QTLS status.

It will also guide you to use the webchat and webinar facilities which are offered by the Society for Education and Training (SET) to its members, and how to obtain online support.

**This chapter will cover the following topics:**

- Role and responsibilities
- Motivation for undertaking QTLS status
- Webchats and webinars
- Online support

# Role and responsibilities

Role and responsibilities is the next section of the workbook which you can begin to complete when you are ready. It's about your teaching career and your current job role.

## Activity

*Access your workbook as before, and go to the* Role and Responsibilities *section by clicking on the* Role and Responsibilities *tab, as in Figure 4.1.*

**Figure 4.1 Accessing the Role and Responsibilities section**

There are two parts to the *Role and Responsibilities* section:

• your teaching career to date and why you became a teacher or trainer (you will need your CV for this section)

• your current role and responsibilities.

Make sure you read all the supporting notes, which appear on the screen regarding this section of your workbook, prior to carrying out the activities.

## Tip

*It's best to make backup copies of any written work which you key directly into the text boxes in your workbook. Alternatively, use a word processor first and then copy and paste your text over. You might also like to create a folder on your computer or device to save copies of all the electronic documents and images you will upload to your workbook.*

## Your teaching career to date and why you became a teacher or trainer

Think of this section as your journey into teaching or training. It doesn't matter when you started, or how you are currently employed, but you must demonstrate you are currently working with learners aged 14 plus (i.e. in years 10, 11 and above) and/or with adults. This can be on a one-to-one basis but you must be able to be observed with a group of learners (five or more) during the professional formation process.

You only have 500 words for this section so you must be succinct and to the point. You might like to make some rough notes first.

## Tip

*You will be able to go under or over any aspect with a defined word-count by 10 per cent. If you are not sure how to calculate your word-count, copy and paste your text into an online checker such as the one at this link:* https://wordcounter.net/

Throughout this section, you can upload any supporting evidence such as:

- your CV

- relevant notes from meetings regarding your responsibilities

- testimonials from managers or mentors regarding your role.

## Activity

*Consider your journey since joining the teaching profession. Include key milestones such as the impact another teacher has had on your practice; someone who has really inspired you; and/or a positive or a negative experience that made you decide to become a teacher. Key in text to the first box on the screen, as in Figure 4.2, in 500 words. You could use a word processor first (or equivalent software) and then copy and paste your text into the box on the screen when you are ready. You can also upload any supporting evidence (assets). Remember to save your work as you progress.*

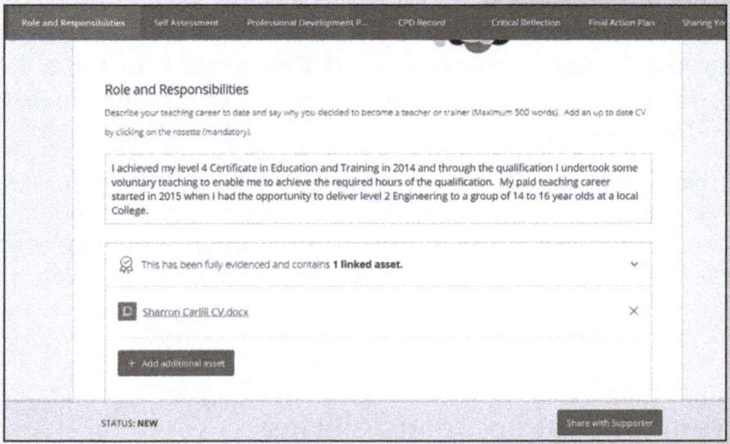

**Figure 4.2 Adding text and assets to describe your teaching career to date**

## Tip

*As you are demonstrating what you have achieved, make sure you write in the first person by using the word 'I'. For example, I achieved…*

If you are confident with your English and writing skills, your responses can be keyed directly into the box on the screen. However, do remember to keep saving your work (the blue button in the top left corner of the screen marked *Save*) so that you don't lose your work. If you would prefer to reflect on what you have written, and check your spelling and grammar, you could use a word processor first (or equivalent software) and then copy and paste your text into the box on the screen.

## Tip

*Different browsers such as Edge, Firefox and Google Chrome can affect the spell checker of the workbook and add symbols to the text (when it is copied and pasted from a word processor). Always double check your work for any inaccuracies.*

You might wish to ask a friend or a colleague to check it for you, just in case you have made any mistakes. You can do this by clicking on *I want to* in the top right-hand corner of your screen. You might also like to make a backup copy of what you have written (if you have keyed directly onto the screen) in case anything happens to your workbook (i.e. you lose the internet connection).

## Activity

*Upload your CV and any other supporting evidence by clicking on the red rosette and choosing* Add an asset. *You can then click on* UPLOAD *to add a document from your device. Once done, you can key in notes in the text box to justify your evidence if you wish.*

*You should then select* This item is now fully evidenced *to change the rosette from amber to green. This will denote you have evidenced this section. You will also be informed how many linked assets you have, i.e. pieces of evidence, as in Figure 4.2. Clicking on the X symbol at the right-hand side will delete your evidence, so do be careful. However, you can re-upload it if necessary.*

## Your current role and responsibilities

This next section is about what you are currently doing as part of your teaching role and responsibilities. You only have 200 words for this so you must be succinct and to the point.

You can also upload any supporting evidence such as:

- your job description

- relevant notes from meetings

- quality improvement/action plans

- documents showing examples of working with external agencies

- documents showing examples of networking with others.

You must demonstrate you are currently working with learners aged 14 plus (i.e. in years 10, 11 and above) and/or with adults. You must also state the type of learner you are teaching, and your subject specialism. If your practice involves different types of subjects and learners, you can include this in your comments. However, you should choose a particular subject and group of learners to base your application on.

For example:

- year 10 in a school environment working towards GCSEs in maths

- 16+ engineering apprentices in the workplace

- 16–18-year-olds working towards a qualification in Customer Service at college, which includes work experience

- 19+ adults taking motor vehicle maintenance at evening classes.

You might like to make notes first or use a word processor. You could also refer to the activities you undertook in Chapter 1 regarding:

- the funding stream your learners fall into

- who else you work with to improve the quality of teaching, learning and assessment in your organisation, and how this positively impacts on your learners.

You must also state how you work with your colleagues to improve the quality of teaching and learning in your organisation. This might include:

- peer observations and feedback

- standardisation of practice

- collaboration with others

- sharing best practice.

Peer observations and feedback enable teachers and trainers to learn from each other in a non-threatening environment. The process can be a very powerful tool in disseminating best practice. This can lead to improvements in quality across the organisation, not only for new teachers, but experienced teachers too.

Standardisation of practice can support teachers and trainers to interpret programme or qualification requirements in the same way, ensuring a consistent experience for all learners.

Collaborating with others, whether in the same organisation or not, can help to improve knowledge and skills.

Sharing best practice enables practitioners to demonstrate and share proven resourceful, inspiring and innovative ideas. These can help to motivate, engage and support learners' progress.

Activities can include:

- internal quality assurers agreeing how staff can be consistent with their practice to support their learners

- carrying out (and visually recording for later viewing and feedback) role play activities such as assessment planning; micro teaching; making a decision; giving feedback; dealing with a complaint: completing records

- chairing/attending meetings to discuss programme/qualification specifications, policies and procedures, regulatory bodies' requirements

- creating interesting assignments, formative and summative assessment activities (based on the programme requirements and at different levels if required) with models of expected answers

- designing and creating innovative delivery and assessment materials

- inspiring learning through the use of new and emerging technologies

- experienced staff observing, mentoring and supporting new staff

- stretching and challenging learning in exciting ways.

If your job role includes the above or any other activities, you could write about this in your statement.

The professional formation process is to help you develop as a teacher/trainer and it is not expected at this stage that you carry out standardisation and best practice activities. These could be areas which you choose to develop as you progress through the professional formation process.

## Activity

*Key in text to the next box on the screen regarding your Current Role and Responsibilities, as in Figure 4.3, in 200 words. You could use a word processor first (or equivalent software) and then copy and paste your text into the box on the screen when you are ready. Remember to save your work as you progress and to upload any supporting documents.*

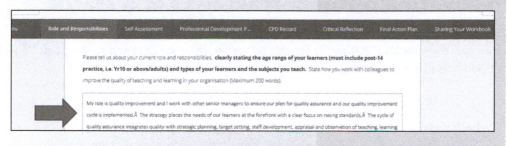

**Figure 4.3 Adding text to describe your current roles and responsibilities**

## Tip

*Don't use any names of learners, colleagues and/or organisations when writing your text. Cover up or mask over names on any supporting evidence prior to uploading. If you are using organisational documents such as templates, get permission from your organisation that it's okay to use them.*

If you have keyed your text directly into the box on the screen, don't forget to create a backup copy by copying and pasting what you have written into a word processor. If you are using a computer and the *copy* and/or *paste* options don't work (perhaps because of the browser you are using) you can try the following:

- to copy – highlight the text to copy and then hold down the CTRL key and tap the letter C

- to paste – move the cursor and click to where you would like the text to appear, then hold down the CTRL key and tap the letter V.

If you make any mistakes and want to undo what you have just done, you can try the following:

- to undo your last action(s) – hold down CTRL and tap the letter Z.

## Activity

*Add any supporting evidence by clicking on the red rosette and uploading it to your workbook (as explained earlier in this chapter). You can add text to the box if you wish, and then choose* This item is now fully evidenced.

# Motivation for undertaking QTLS status

This section is about the reason why you are undertaking QTLS status, i.e. what has motivated you. You only have 200 words for this so you must be succinct and to the point. You can also upload any supporting evidence such as documents relating to:

- a promotion at work which requires you to hold QTLS status

- the chance of a new teaching job which requires you to hold QTLS status

- an appraisal from your supervisor which recommends that you achieve QTLS status

- evidence of research you have undertaken to demonstrate the positive impact that holding QTLS status can have on your organisation.

## Activity

*Look back at the activity you completed in Chapter 1 regarding* What is motivating me to be the best I can be? *This will help you complete this section. Key in text to the* Motivation for Undertaking QTLS *box, as in Figure 4.4, in 200 words. You could use a word processor first (or equivalent software) and then copy and paste your text into the box on the screen when you are ready. Remember to save your work as you progress and to upload any supporting documents. You can add text to the box if you wish to justify your evidence, and then choose* This item is now fully evidenced.

You might like to makes notes first or use a word processor, and don't forget that you can ask a friend or a colleague to check your work. When you are writing, try to consider what impact achieving QTLS will have on you, your learners and your organisation.

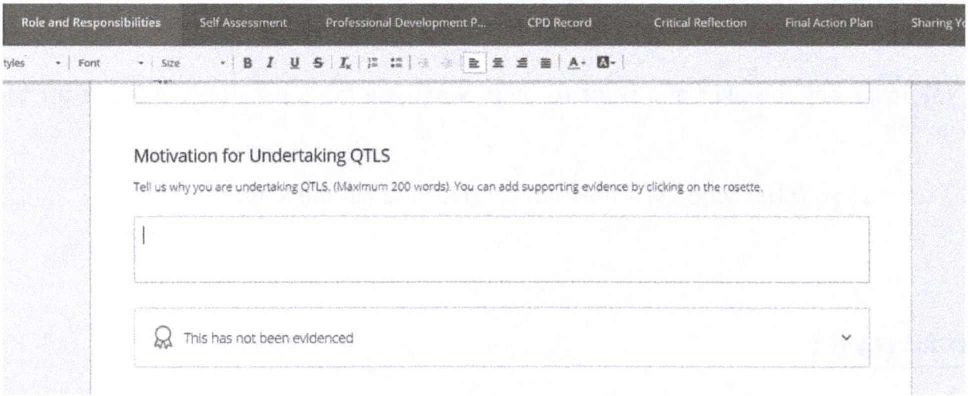

**Figure 4.4 Adding text to describe your motivation for undertaking QTLS**

*Make sure you have clicked on Save in the top left corner of the screen. Then tick the box at the end of the page to* Mark page as complete *(once you are sure it is all completed).*

You can now log out of your workbook or progress to the next section which is covered in the following chapter.

# Webchats and webinars

A webchat is a way of communicating with others and a webinar is a presentation or seminar. They are offered in real time and are online; however, you can access a transcript of a copy of the presentation afterwards. They are really useful ways of partaking in continuing professional development (CPD) and networking with others.

SET offer the following to members throughout the year, regarding various topics such as:

- 16–18 performance tables
- digital tools for communication and collaboration
- dual professionalism
- maths: taking on the challenge
- mindfulness for learners and practitioners
- QTLS: your questions answered
- supporting deaf or visually impaired young people in FE
- working effectively with support staff.

*Take a look at the webchat events which are scheduled, or access a transcript of previous ones at this link: https://tinyurl.com/SETwebchats*

*You can see details of all the previous webinars at this link: https://tinyurl.com/SETwebinars. You will need to log in to access them.*

## Live chat service

SET offers online support to individuals wanting to undertake QTLS status in the form of a live chat. Key personnel from SET will respond to you in real time. This includes a panel of experts – for example, the Head of QTLS status, the Operations Manager and relevant administrators. You can key in questions and a member of the panel will answer and give appropriate guidance. The live chat service is part of SET's commitment to provide support and information to their members, as well as engaging with those who are interested in finding out more about becoming a member.

The live chat service enables members and non-members to submit questions and feedback in real time, but is not accessible from your workbook; it is accessible via the following SET website pages:

- Membership form

- QTLS eligibility criteria

- Become a member

- SET dashboard (members only).

When the service is available you will see the live chat icon, as in Figure 4.5, in the bottom right-hand corner of the screen, on the above SET webpages.

**Figure 4.5  Live chat icon**

Once you have clicked on the live chat icon, you will be asked to complete a text box detailing your name, email address and telephone number before being put through to someone from the membership enquires team.

After the live chat session, you will be able to give feedback of one to five stars regarding the support you received.

# Online support

As you progress through the professional formation process, never feel you are on your own. There are various online support networks via social media which you could join. You will find members there who will be experiencing the same issues as you and it would be good to communicate with them.

| Activity |
| --- |

*If you have access to Facebook and/or LinkedIn, you could join one or more of the following groups to post questions and gain support from members:*

*https://www.facebook.com/groups/SETQTLS/*

*https://www.facebook.com/groups/FEandSkills/*

*https://www.linkedin.com/groups/4942272*

No matter what your question might be, or how silly you think it might be, there are bound to be others experiencing the same. Don't be afraid to ask your question in any of the above group forums or to respond to questions posted by others.

SET also has a Facebook page which you might like to follow to keep up to date with their activities: https://www.facebook.com/SocEducationTraining/

Throughout the professional formation process, you might find it useful to have a buddy or a mentor, in addition to your supporter. This person doesn't have to be someone you work with, they could be a colleague or friend, or someone you get to know via one of the online support groups. They could help you stay motivated and give you encouragement to keep going when you might feel like giving up.

## Contacting SET

If you need to contact SET, you can do so in the following ways. Please include your membership number when getting in touch, and clearly state what your query is about.

Email:

- membership enquiries – membership.enquiries@etfoundation.co.uk

- technical enquires regarding your workbook – technical@etfoundation.co.uk

SET aims to respond to your email within five working days.

Telephone:

- phone (free phone): 0800 093 9111

- phone (local call): 020 3092 5001

Phone lines are open Monday to Friday, 9 am to 8 pm. Hours may change during public and bank holidays.

Mail:

>The Society for Education and Training
>
>157–197 Buckingham Palace Road
>
>London
>
>SW1W 9SP.

---

### Tip

*If you forget your SET password you can reset this online at this link: https://tiny url.com/ybpftovc. You will need your email address or membership number, and your surname and date of birth.*

## Summary

This chapter has explored how to complete the second stage of your workbook. This included inputting information regarding your role and responsibilities, and your motivation for undertaking QTLS status. It also introduced you to the webchat and webinar facilities which are offered by SET to its members, and how to obtain online support.

You might like to carry out further research by accessing the books and websites listed at the end of this chapter.

This chapter has covered the following topics:

* Role and responsibilities

* Motivation for undertaking QTLS status

* Webchats and webinars

* Online support

## References and further information

Crawley, J (2018) *Just Teach! in FE: A People-Centred Approach*. London: Learning Matters.

Gravells, A. (2017) *Principles and Practices of Teaching and Training*. London: SAGE/Learning Matters

Petty, G., (2009) *Evidence-based Teaching: A Practical Approach* (2nd edition). Cheltenham: Nelson Thornes.

Tummons, J. (2010) *Becoming a Professional Tutor* (2nd edition). Exeter: Learning Matters.

# Websites

Education and Training Foundation (ETF) – www.et-foundation.co.uk

Society for Education and Training (SET) – https://set.et-foundation.co.uk

SET Webchats – https://tinyurl.com/SETwebchats

SET Webinars – https://tinyurl.com/SETwebinars

Word-counter – https://wordcounter.net

# 5

# Self-assessment

## Introduction

This chapter will assist you in completing the third stage of your online portfolio by asking you to work through various activities.

It will explain how to undertake the self-assessment process using the online tool provided in your workbook. The benefit of self-assessment is that it can benchmark your starting point with a view to improving your practice.

It will also guide you regarding how to prepare for and undertake your first mandatory observation. In addition, it will explain how to embed aspects of the Minimum Core during your lessons.

**This chapter will cover the following topics:**

- Self-assessment
- Preparing for an observation
- Observation report
- The Minimum Core

# Self-assessment

Self-assessment is the next section of the workbook which you can begin to complete when you are ready. The self-assessment process enables you to assess your practice in relation to the Professional Standards using an online self-assessment tool.

The Professional Standards are based on three areas:

- Professional values and attributes

- Professional knowledge and understanding

- Professional skills

which will be explained later in this chapter.

The self-assessment process enables you to reflect on your practice, which is about helping you become more self-aware. This should give you increased confidence and improve the links between the theory and practice of teaching, learning and assessment. It should become a part of your everyday activities, enabling you to analyse and focus on things in greater detail. All reflection should lead to an improvement in practice. However, there may be events you would not want to change or improve as you felt they went well. If this is the case, reflect as to *why* they went well and use your thoughts to improve future lessons.

Reflective practice should take place after every lesson, not just the ones when you are observed. As you become more experienced with reflective practice, you will progress from thoughts of *I didn't do that very well*, to aspects of more significance such as *why* you didn't do it very well and *how* you could change something as a result. You may realise you need further training or support in some areas, therefore partaking in relevant continuing professional development (CPD) could help. As a result, you might find your own skills improving, for example giving more effective, constructive and developmental feedback to your learners. CPD is explained in Chapter 6.

## Online self-assessment tool

The online self-assessment process will take you a minimum of one hour of undisturbed time. It's not something you can start and then come back to, it must all be completed in one session, otherwise you will lose what you have done (as the online form cannot be saved part way through). You will need to totally focus on answering the questions related to each of the 20 Professional Standards, as in Appendix 1.

## Tip

*Page 15 onwards of the document* Initial Guidance for users of the Professional Standards *gives examples for each of them. https://tinyurl.com/y9pprxgd*

It is a mandatory requirement to include reflective comments as you answer each question, which will help you identify areas for your own development. This is an opportunity to also make links to your organisation's development, and to recognise how you can collaborate with others to further improve your own practice. There is no option to complete the questions and then go back at a later date to add your reflective comments, therefore the online tool must be completed fully before saving.

## Tip

*You might like to use a word processor first to key in your text and then copy and paste it to your workbook once you are happy with it. This way you can work through it in stages. If you key directly into the online form and don't complete it all in one session, you will not be able to save it.*

The spellchecker should highlight any spelling errors by underlining them in red, but the browser you use may affect this. Do fully proof read your work and ensure any errors are corrected before saving. Once completed, the document will be saved as a portable document file (PDF) which does not allow any amendments to be made to it afterwards.

## Activity

*Access your workbook as before, and go to the Self-assessment section by clicking on the Self-Assessment tab. Read the text on the screen, then click on the Self-Assessment Tool text, as in Figure 5.1. Make sure you have at least an hour to complete the self-assessment tool.*

**Figure 5.1 Accessing the self-assessment tool through your workbook**

Once you have opened the self-assessment tool, your name, membership number and the date will be prepopulated onto page 1 of the form; if they are not, you can add them, as in Figure 5.2. The tool is opened in a new window, so your workbook will still be open in another window if you need to go back to it.

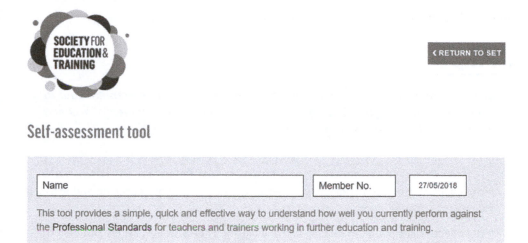

**Figure 5.2 Page 1 of the self-assessment tool**

Each question on the self-assessment tool requires you to score yourself on a sliding scale between 0 and 6. A score of 1 indicates you are just meeting the standard and a score of 6 indicates you are performing well against the standard. To set your score, click on the grey slider (currently above 0) and, keeping your mouse pressed down, drag the slider to the required number, then release. To help you assess your performance against each question, text will appear below the score bar for each number chosen. Remember to add reflective comments in the text box to support your assessment score as it is a mandatory require-ment. Once you have completed the tool, no other comments can be added. A sentence or two is fine for each; remember to carefully check your spelling and grammar.

## Tip

*Unlike competencies which you either have or you do not have, performance against standards can be developed over time. You may feel you are already per-forming satisfactorily in some areas, whereas others will need developing. It's best to choose to work on the standards that are most relevant to your practice, your learners and your organisation and to be honest with your responses.*

*Professional values and attributes*

The first section of the self-assessment tool focuses on your *Professional values and attrib-utes*, as in Figure 5.3. This section supports you in developing your own judgement of what works well and what does not work well regarding your teaching and training role.

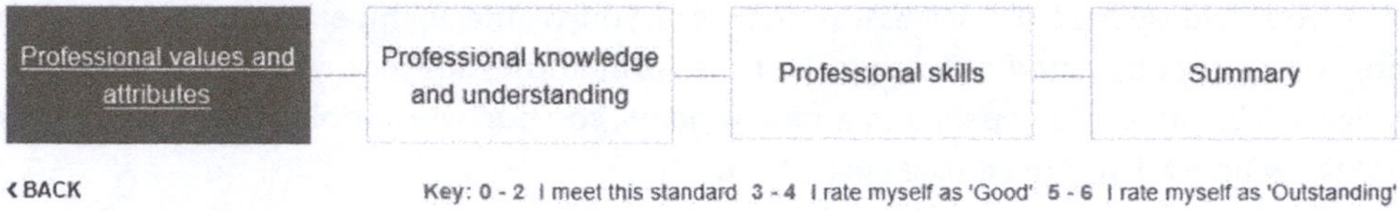

| Professional values and attributes | Professional knowledge and understanding | Professional skills | Summary |

‹ BACK                    Key: 0 - 2  I meet this standard  3 - 4  I rate myself as 'Good'  5 - 6  I rate myself as 'Outstanding'

**Figure 5.3  Self-assessment: Professional values and attributes**

## Activity

*Answer the following six questions using the slider on the self-assessment tool to add your score, as in Figure 5.4, and include your reflective comments. You can click each of the numbered scores for hints to appear.*

1. How effective are you at reflecting on what works best in your teaching and learning to meet the diverse needs of learners?

2. How effective are you at evaluating and challenging your practice, values and beliefs?

3. How effective are you at inspiring, motivating and raising aspirations of learners through your enthusiasm and knowledge?

4. How creative and innovative are you in selecting and adapting strategies to help learners to learn?

5. How much do you value and promote social and cultural diversity, equality of opportunity and inclusion?

6. How effective are you at building positive and collaborative relationships with colleagues and learners?

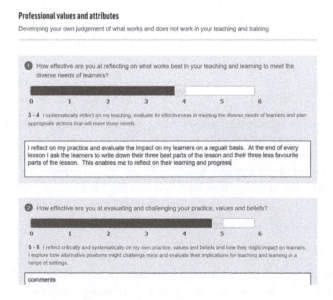

**Figure 5.4  Self-assessment questions sample: Professional values and attributes**

*Professional knowledge and understanding*

The second section of the self-assessment tool focuses on your *Professional knowledge and understanding*. This section supports you in developing deep and critical informed knowledge and understanding of theory and practice – in other words, further developing what you know and can do.

## Activity

*Click on the Professional knowledge and understanding tab. Answer the following six questions using the slider on the self-assessment tool to add your score, and include your reflective comments.*

7. How effective are you at maintaining and updating knowledge of your subject and/or vocational area?

8. How effective are you at maintaining and updating your knowledge of educational research to develop evidence-based practice?

9. How effective are you at applying theoretical understanding of effective practice in teaching, learning and assessment, drawing on research and other evidence?

10. How effective are you at evaluating your practice with others and assessing its impact on learning?

11. How effective are you at managing and promoting positive learner behaviour?

12. How well do you understand the teaching and professional role and your responsibilities?

*Professional skills*

The third section of the self-assessment tool focuses on your *Professional skills*. This section supports you in developing your expertise and skills to ensure the best outcome for learners.

Outcomes for learners could include:

- achievement

- meeting the needs of diverse groups or individuals

- promoting the use of technology

- working creatively to overcome individual learner's barriers to maths or English

- enabling learners to be accountable for their own learning to support their progress

- progression into employment or higher levels of learning.

## Activity

*Click on the* Professional skills *tab. Answer the following eight questions using the slider on the self-assessment tool to add your score, and include your reflective comments.*

13. How effective are you at motivating and inspiring learners to promote achievement and develop their skills to enable progression?

14. How effective are you at planning and delivering effective learning programmes for diverse groups or individuals in a safe and inclusive environment?

15. How effective are you at promoting the benefits of technology and supporting learners in its use?

16. How effective are you at addressing the mathematics and English needs of learners and working creatively to overcome individual barriers to learning?

17. How effective are you at enabling learners to share responsibility for their own learning and assessment, setting goals that stretch and challenge?

18. How effective are you at applying appropriate and fair methods of assessment and providing constructive and timely feedback to support progression and achievement?

19. How effective are you at maintaining and updating your teaching and training expertise and vocational skills through collaboration with employers?

20. How effective are you contributing to organisational development and quality improvement through collaboration with others?

### Self-assessment Summary

Once you have completed the questions you can click on the *Summary* tab for a self-assessment overview of each of the three areas of the Professional Standards, as in Figure 5.5.

Scroll down to see each section, which will have a diagram on the left-hand side showing your profile and your scores. Your scores and text are on the right-hand side. This overview will enable you to identify areas for your development. You will need to include your areas for development in your *Professional Development Plan* which will be explained in Chapter 6. It's important to save your summary as you will need to upload it to your workbook; it's not saved automatically. *Export to PDF* is the term used to save it.

## Activity

*Scroll down to where you can see the* Combined summary *and click on the* Export to PDF *button, as in Figure 5.6. This will enable you to view your document in a new window on the screen. You must then save it (by right clicking on it and choosing* Save as) *to your computer or device. You can also print it by right clicking on it and choosing* Print.

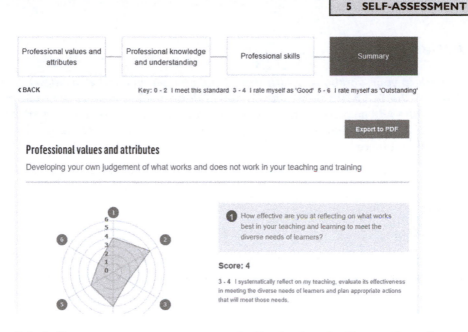

## Figure 5.5 Self-assessment summary sample: Professional values and attributes

> ### Tip
>
> *If you don't save it, you will lose it. Make sure you save it with a name you will remember, and in a place you can access again when you are ready to upload it to your workbook.*

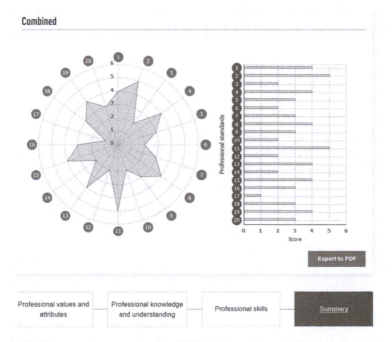

## Figure 5.6 Self-assessment combined summary, and saving your work as a PDF document

## Activity

*Go back to your workbook (which should still be open in another window). Scroll down to the* Self-Assessment *section and click on the red rosette. You can now click on the* Add an asset *button and upload your self-assessment document, as in Figure 5.7. You can add text to the box if you wish, and then choose* This item is now fully evidenced.

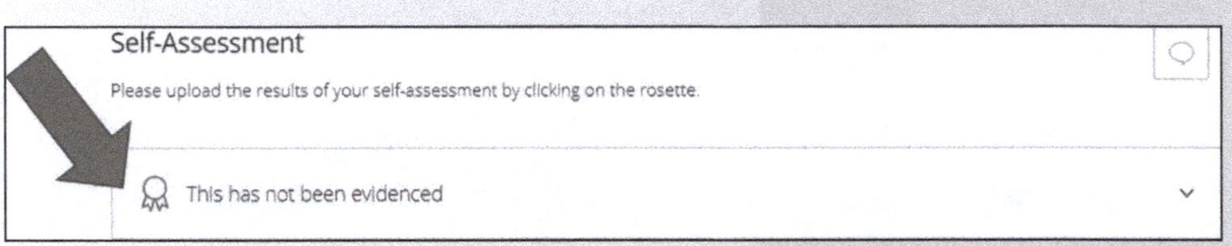

Figure 5.7 **Uploading your self-assessment document to your workbook**

Once you have uploaded it to your workbook, you can close the self-assessment windows which are still open.

## Tip

*At certain points throughout your workbook, you will see a speech bubble icon: ⊙ You can click on it to add comments, for example, if you would like to clarify anything for the person who will review your evidence.*

# Preparing for an observation

You will be formally observed on at least two occasions throughout the time you are working towards QTLS status. Your evidence for this will need to be uploaded to the next part of the Self-assessment section of your workbook. You will need to come back later to this section of your workbook if you haven't been observed yet.

The first mandatory observation must be undertaken within one month of the date you registered for the professional formation process. The second mandatory observation should be no more than one month before submitting your workbook. There should be at least three months between them. Your observed practice must be demonstrated with learners aged 14 plus (i.e. in years 10, 11 and above) and/or with adults.

If you miss the one month deadline for your first observation, you must make sure your final observation is at least three months afterwards, and before the deadline for submitting your workbook to the Society for Education and Training (SET).

## Activity

*Plan ahead now and arrange the dates and times for your two observations with your supporter. Remember that the first observation must be within one month of the date you registered and the second should be at least three months later.*

The observations can be by your supporter and/or someone you work closely with, such as your manager or a mentor. The feedback you receive will help you to identify areas that will inform your professional development plan (PDP).

You cannot use any observation documents which are from your initial teaching qualification, or from any other situation. It would be useful for you to be observed by one of your peers prior to being formally observed. They might give you some valuable feedback. You could also observe one of their lessons, where you might gain some new ideas. Peer observations are a useful part of your CPD.

The time length of each observation should ideally be one hour (or more) and you will need to agree a suitable date and time well in advance with your observer. SET does not accept *learning walks*, i.e. observations which are really just a short snapshot of what is taking place or which only take 15–20 minutes. Ideally, you should be observed for a minimum of 60 minutes or the full length of the lesson you are delivering.

## Activity

*Ask your supporter (or whoever will observe you) if you can see a copy of the form they will complete when they observe you. The form is not supplied by SET, so they might use their own, or the one your organisation uses for the observation of teaching and learning.*

*Double check the date and time you will be observed, and partake in the observation when you are ready.*

Your observer will be looking to satisfy themselves that you are using teaching, learning and assessment approaches and activities effectively. They will want to see that learning is taking place, and that you are including all your learners during the lesson and differentiating for any particular needs. They will probably use the organisation's observation document which you might already be familiar with. They must comment on your strengths as well as your areas for your development. This will help you produce your PDP.

## Final checks prior to your observation

Make sure all the materials you have prepared are of good quality, are varied, address inclusivity and differentiation, and are free from spelling, grammar and punctuation errors.

Don't try and prepare too much and risk showing off, or use any equipment you are not totally comfortable with. Make sure you have a spare activity in case you have extra time available, and extension activities to stretch and challenge learners when necessary. Always have a contingency plan, i.e. hard copies of an electronic presentation in case of an equipment malfunction. You could also consider which activities you could reduce or remove if you are running out of time. Check the environment and equipment beforehand, and complete any health and safety checks and risk assessments. Make sure you have enough materials for the number of learners you expect, plus a spare for your observer.

Your lesson plan should show a clear aim (what you want to achieve) and objectives or tasks which your learners will carry out. You should also state how you will check that learning will take place, i.e. the different assessment methods you will use. If possible, it would be useful to ask your observer to comment on your lesson plan well before the observation takes place.

Above all, don't panic, keep calm and don't try to do too much. You are still learning, and you will need to work at things over time. If you make a mistake, it's fine and it shows you are human. Just be honest with yourself and learn from it.

It's extremely useful to SET, when it reviews your documents, if the following are included as part of your lesson plan:

- course title
- date, time and location
- number of learners
- age range (if teaching in a school)
- topic.

### Activity

*Have a look at the lesson plan you will use for your observation; it should be one you normally use at work. Ensure it covers the points in the previous bullet list and prepare it ready for use.*

## During the observation

Being observed, even if you are an experienced teacher, can be a bit worrying or stressful, as you will want to deliver a perfect lesson. However, you are being observed every time you deliver a lesson by your own learners, it's just that they don't always give you feedback afterwards. For your observed lessons, you will need to obtain feedback from your learners, which is explained later in this chapter.

You might want to give your observer some details of your individual learners, perhaps in the form of a group profile. This will show how you will be differentiating to meet their individual needs, along with strategies to support them. Your observer may also want to see your record of attendance/register, and other relevant administrative documents. These might be electronic rather than hard copies, but they should still be accessible.

You might want to inform your learners in advance that the lesson is to be observed, and that you expect them to behave in their usual way. Otherwise, they might feel they should be quiet, not ask any questions, or ask too many questions to appear helpful, which will give a false impression of what normally occurs. Your observer may want to talk to your learners at some point, and might ask you to leave the room whilst they do this. Don't be concerned, this is quite normal; they like to find out what your learners are experiencing and how your teaching is having an impact upon their learning.

## Tip

*If you are nervous, don't let your learners know, as they probably won't notice. There's also no need to tell your observer, as they will be expecting you to be confident at what you do. You are human though and, if you make a mistake, your observer will be watching to see that you put it right.*

You could introduce your observer to your learners at the beginning and state they are observing the lesson, not them as individuals. Having a stranger in the room might lead to some behaviour issues if you haven't forewarned your learners. If so, you must deal with these as soon as they arise and do it in a professional manner. Just be yourself. If you are asked a question by a learner which you don't know the answer to, say you will find out afterwards, and then make sure that you do.

Try not to look at your observer whilst they are with you, they are not part of your group and will not participate in any activities. Don't embarrass them by trying to involve them. They will be making lots of notes throughout the lesson; therefore, try not to be concerned if they don't appear to be watching you all the time, they will still be listening to what's going on. If you can, forget that they are there and ignore them; your learners should be the focus of your lesson, not your observer.

Keep your lesson plan handy either as a hard copy or on an electronic device. You could highlight key points which you can glance at quickly to make sure you are on track. Don't worry if you don't follow your lesson plan exactly. As your lesson progresses you will naturally adapt the timings and activities. Your observer will not mind if you don't keep to your timings as it will show you are being flexible to meet the needs of your learners.

Ensure your learners are engaged throughout and that learning is taking place. Ask lots of open questions to different learners (by name) to check their knowledge. You could have a list of your learners' names and tick them off once you have asked a question. This is fine if your group is not too large, and it keeps a check on how you have included each learner. Try and use a variety of teaching and learning approaches and activities to stretch and challenge your learners. If possible, use technology to support the teaching and learning process. Above all, make sure learning has taken place. If you are not using formal assessment activities, make sure you use informal activities which will enable your learners to demonstrate the progress they have made during the lesson.

### Tip

*You may find that you finish earlier than you had planned. If so, make sure you have a pre-prepared spare activity you could use. Depending upon the level of your learners, you could give them a crossword, a multiple-choice quiz, or they could hold a small group or paired discussion regarding the pros and cons of a relevant topic. Whatever you do, don't forget to check how much learning is taking place.*

At the end of your lesson you will need to confirm what has been learnt by linking to the objectives or tasks. You can then explain what will be covered during the next lesson (if applicable) and set any homework or other activities to be carried out during self-study time. Always plan to finish on time, otherwise your learners might decide to leave before you have completed. If the room needs to be left tidy, involve your learners in this before the lesson finishes. You can then talk to your observer after your learners have left, providing time has been arranged for this.

## After the observation

If your observer stays until the end of your lesson, they should be able to give you verbal feedback when your learners have left. If this is not possible, make sure you ask your observer when you will receive their feedback, which might be verbal, electronic or paper-based. Ideally, the feedback should be given in a quiet area which will enable you to listen and focus upon what is said. You might also like to make some notes. Don't be afraid of asking your observer to pause whilst you make them. There will be a lot of information to take in, and they might be happy for you to digitally record the feedback so that you can listen to it again later.

Hopefully, the feedback you receive will reassure you that you are teaching correctly, and that learning is taking place. However, if you receive some negative feedback don't take it personally, your observer has only seen a snapshot of what you are capable of.

Your observer might have identified some points for your further training and development which you hadn't considered. This will be helpful when you create your PDP. Don't forget to get a copy of their observation report (which they must have signed and dated) as you will need to upload it to your workbook. If it is not signed, it will not be accepted when SET reviews your workbook.

*The minimum evidence you should upload regarding your observed practice is:*

- *First observation: lesson plan and observation report (signed and dated by your observer and you)*

- *Final observation: lesson plan; observation report (signed and dated by your observer and you) and your self-evaluation report (which should make reference to learner feedback and will be covered later in this chapter).*

*However, you can upload more supporting documents if you wish, such as further observations, a scheme of work, a group profile, and evidence of feedback from your learners.*

# Observation report

There are two mandatory observation reports required for your teaching, learning and assessment practice; however, you can be observed more than twice if you wish. The first report is evidence for the *Self-assessment* section of your workbook and the second is for the *Critical reflection* section.

The observation report must be signed and dated by the person who observed you, as well as yourself. This could be your supporter, a manager, your mentor or a colleague. A copy of each of the completed signed observation reports should be uploaded to the relevant section of your workbook as part of the mandatory evidence.

**Tip**

*Make sure your observer signs and dates the observation report and gives you a hard copy or an electronic copy (saved to a place where you are able to access it). You will need to upload the reports to your workbook. An electronic signature is acceptable in the form of an email address.*

If you are teaching on a one-to-one basis, it is possible to use evidence from this practice for your professional formation. However, you must be able to produce evidence in your workbook of at least one observation from teaching a group (five or more learners).

**Tip**

*The evidence for each observation does not have to be from the same group of learners. If you predominantly teach on a one-to-one basis, one observation must be with groups (five or more learners). Both observations should be at least three months apart.*

Any feedback from your learners, the observation report form, and your self-evaluation of the lesson should be used along with your self-assessment results to inform your professional development plan (explained in Chapter 6).

## Activity

*Once you have been observed and have the necessary evidence, scroll down to the* Observation Report *section of the* Self-Assessment *page of your workbook. Click on the red rosette. Then click on the* Add an asset *button and upload your observation report. You can add text to the box if you wish, and then choose* This item is now fully evidenced.

You can upload additional evidence besides your observation report. For example a scheme of work and learning materials. If you wish, you can refer to a piece of evidence you have previously uploaded, when completing other sections of your workbook.

## Activity

*Tick the box at the end of the page to* Mark page as complete *(once you are sure it is all completed).*

## Self-evaluation

Self-evaluation is a way of continually thinking about your own practice to ensure you are carrying out your role effectively. When evaluating your practice, you will need to consider how your own behaviour has impacted upon others, what you could do to improve and then consider ways of putting this into practice. The word *self* would make you think that you need to do it on your own. However, what you think and what others think might be quite different. If you self-evaluate that you have delivered a fantastic lesson as none of your learners fell asleep, this might be very different to what they actually experienced. When you carry out the self-evaluation process, you should consider the perspectives of your learners. This will help you become more objective with your judgements of yourself, rather than being subjective, i.e. only taking your point of view into consideration.

You should write a self-evaluation report after each observation. SET does not provide a template for this, you can use your organisation's if there is one (perhaps it's part of your lesson plan) or design your own.

Some questions to ask yourself as part of the self-evaluation process could include:

* How well did I plan and prepare my lesson?

* How well did I perform and how did I feel about what I did?

- What went well, what didn't go well and why?

- Did I use a variety of teaching and learning approaches?

- How did I check that learning was taking place?

- Were my learners motivated and actively engaged with the topics?

- Did I meet all the aspects my observer was looking for? If not, how can I meet them, or exceed them next time?

- What have I found out about myself?

- What happened that wasn't meant to happen, and how did I deal with it?

- How were my timings compared to those on my lesson plan?

- If I was to deliver this same lesson again, what would I change and why?

- What can I improve upon and why?

---

### Tip

*You might find it useful to ask yourself the questions in the bullet list after every lesson, not just after your observed lesson. You could even add them to the end of your lesson plan. Make sure you are honest, there's no point being otherwise as you will only be misleading yourself.*

---

The self-evaluation report must include reference to feedback you have gained from your learners. The feedback could be from the results of a questionnaire which you have given to your learners. This could be after:

- an activity

- a unit or a topic area

- the lesson.

### Learner feedback – questionnaires

A questionnaire is a way of gathering information and data which usually involves verbal or written questions given to an individual. When designing a questionnaire, you will need to consider what you want to find out, who you will ask, when you will do it and why. Don't just ask questions for the sake of it, and don't just give them to those you know will give you a positive response; they should be given to all your learners who attended the lesson. You should also take ethics into consideration to ensure no harm comes to anyone as a result of what you will do or will ask. Your organisation should be able to give you advice regarding this.

All your learners should be given the opportunity to be involved and then left to decide if they wish to respond or not. You will also need to consider the timing. If you allow time towards the end of your lesson for your learners to complete their responses, they are more likely to complete them than if you give them a date in the future to complete and return them. Alternatively, you could create a confidential online questionnaire, either to be completed during the lesson, or within an agreed time frame after the lesson.

Anonymity for those completing could lead to you gaining more truthful responses if the person knows they will not be identified. Electronic questionnaires that are emailed back to you will denote who the respondent is; however, postal ones will not (unless a reference code has been added to them). There are lots of online programs and apps which can be used that will guarantee anonymity and will also analyse the results for you. Some of these offer a free basic service such as www.surveymonkey.com.

Make sure you thank your learners for their contributions. Always inform your learners afterwards how their feedback has led to changes and improvements. If the latter have not yet taken place, let your learners know what will happen and when. This will make them feel included and that their responses are valued.

*Question techniques*

When devising questions, you will need to gauge the language and level to suit your learners' ability and age range. The type of question is also crucial as to the amount of information you need to obtain, as is the type of response you expect. Using a *closed* question, i.e. a question only requiring a *yes* or *no* response, will not give you as much information as an *open* question, which enables learners to give a detailed answer.

Open questions begin with *who, what, when, where, why* and *how* (WWWWWH) and they will help ensure you gain good quality answers. If you would rather use closed questions with *yes* or *no* responses, you could ask a further question to enable the learner to elaborate on why they answered *yes* or *no*.

Below are some *yes* or *no* sample statements which you could ask your learners in a questionnaire. Alternatively, you could you use smiley faces, such as: ☺ ☺ ☹ for learners to circle. If you would like further feedback, you could include a comment stating 'please explain your answer'.

- My classes start and finish on time

- I feel motivated to learn

- My teacher is inspiring and knows their subject well

- I have the opportunity to ask questions and clarify points

- Teaching and assessment is challenging and helps me reach my full potential

- I am improving my maths and English as part of my course

- I feel able to contribute to discussions and take part in activities

- I am challenged to reach my full potential

- I am exceeding my targets

- My teacher is always prepared for lessons and is well organised

- My teacher deals with behaviour issues promptly

- I feel I am developing knowledge and skills which will help me in the future

- The course is meeting my expectations

*Design a short questionnaire which you could use with your learners after one of your lessons. Consider what information you would like to know and why, and then devise your questions carefully. You could use a free online program such as www. surveymonkey.com. If you have the opportunity, use it with a group of learners as a pilot, prior to your observed lesson, to see how it works. Remember to set a target date for the return of the responses if it's not completed immediately. Keep a summary of the responses to upload to your workbook as additional evidence.*

# The Minimum Core

The Minimum Core is the term given to aspects which every teacher should know, understand and be able to use. You will have had to demonstrate them whilst working towards a teaching qualification in England. It was originally introduced in 2007 by Lifelong Learning UK and updated by the Education and Training Foundation (ETF) in 2016.

The terms used for the Minimum Core are:

- numeracy

- language and literacy

- information and communication technology (ICT)

however, the terms more widely used now are:

- maths

- English

- digital literacy.

If you don't possess good knowledge and skills in these areas, you may have difficulty supporting the developmental needs of your learners. It might be that your qualifications in these areas were achieved many years ago. Demonstrating these skills whilst you are being observed is a way to show your skills are still current. You need to prove you are qualified to at least level 2 in maths and English as part of the professional formation process.

You might like to take additional learning programmes, perhaps if you need to develop your digital skills or you feel your spelling and grammar need to be improved. When you are teaching, your learners will trust and believe you. If you spell words incorrectly, your learners might think the spelling is correct just because you are their teacher and they expect you to be right.

If you are not competent or confident with the Minimum Core skills, you might be making errors and not know any different. When planning your lessons, consider how you will demonstrate the skills. Also consider which skills you want your learners to demonstrate, for example, the use of English when they are writing. When reviewing their work, you can comment on any errors of spelling, grammar and punctuation to help your learners improve.

## Demonstrating the Minimum Core skills

Your job role will naturally include using the Minimum Core skills.

For example:

### Maths

- analysing and presenting statistical information correctly

- calculating marks and grades correctly

- calculating the correct numbers of resources for the group

- creating mathematical problem solving tasks

- ensuring that learners meet any time constraints

- timing how long presentations and activities will take;

### English

- communicating with learners (verbally and non-verbally)

- creating and using interactive learning resources such as quizzes, crosswords or word searches

- giving explanations and descriptions

- listening and responding to learners

- using spelling, punctuation and grammar correctly

- summarising and clarifying information

- using appropriate language

- writing, e.g. on the board; on flipcharts; on OHP transparencies; in visual presentations, handouts, reports and documents; and when providing feedback;

### Digital literacy

- creating videos, podcasts, blogs and vlogs for your specialist subject

- keeping up to date with your specialist subject area by using the internet and digital resources

- producing learning materials by using technology

- receiving, assessing and giving feedback regarding learners' work which has been submitted electronically

- recording discussions with a smart phone or audio device

- using digital devices, computers and smart phones to support teaching, learning and assessment

- using email to communicate with learners and others

- using ICT for electronic presentations and/or using an interactive whiteboard

- using online programs to check for plagiarism in learners' work

- using social media in an appropriate way

- using the internet for research

- using various devices, programs and apps with learners

- using virtual learning environments (VLEs) such as Moodle to support learning.

## Activity

*Take a look at the following links to access free courses and further information to help you improve your Minimum Core skills. You will need to create an account (if you haven't already done so) and log in.*

*Maths and English – https://tinyurl.com/zfga56h*

*Digital skills – https://tinyurl.com/y9j6jb7c and https://tinyurl.com/ycnps55h*

# Summary

This chapter has explored how to complete the third stage of your workbook. This included how to undertake the self-assessment process using the online tool. Preparing for and undergoing observations have also been explained, as well as how to embed the Minimum Core during your lessons.

You might like to carry out further research by accessing the books and websites listed at the end of this chapter.

This chapter has covered the following topics:

- Self-assessment

- Preparing for an observation

- Observation report

- The Minimum Core

# References and further information

Brookfield, S. D. (2017) *Becoming a Critically Reflective Teacher*. San Francisco: Jossey Bass.

Duckworth, V., Wood, J., Dickinson, J. and Bostock, J. (2010) *Successful Teaching Practice in the Lifelong Learning Sector*. Exeter: Learning Matters.

ETF (2016) *Minimum Core Guidance*. London: Education and Training Foundation.

Gregson, M. and Hillier, Y. (2015) *Reflective Teaching in Further, Adult and Vocational Education*. London: Bloomsbury.

Kirkpatrick, D. (1994, 2006) *Evaluating Training Programs*. Oakland: Berrett-Koehler.

O'Leary, M. (2016) *Reclaiming Lesson Observation: Supporting Excellence in Teacher Learning*. Abingdon: Routledge.

O'Leary, M. (2013) *Classroom Observation: A Guide to the Effective Observation of Teaching and Learning*. Abingdon: Routledge.

Peart, S. and Atkins, L. (2011) *Teaching 14–19 Learners in the Lifelong Learning Sector*. Exeter: Learning Matters.

Race, P. and Pickford, R. (2007) *Making Teaching Work*. London: SAGE.

Roffey-Barentsen, J. and Malthouse, R. (2013) *Reflective Practice in Education and Training* (2nd edition). London: Learning Matters.

Rushton, I. and Suter, M. (2012) *Reflective Practice for Teaching in Lifelong Learning*. Maidenhead: OU Press.

Sellars, M. (2017) *Reflective Practice for Teachers*. London: SAGE.

Sharnock, T. (2018) *Using Lesson Observation to Improve Learning: Practical Strategies for FE and Post-16 Tutors*. Northwich: Critical.

Tripp, D. (2012) *Critical Incidents in Teaching: Developing Professional Judgement*. London: Routledge.

Wood, J. and Dickinson, J. (2011) *Quality Assurance and Evaluation in the Lifelong Learning Sector*. Exeter: Learning Matters.

# Websites

Computer free support – www.learnmyway.com/subjects

Digital Unite computer support – http://digitalunite.com/guides

Education and Training Foundation Minimum Core Guidance (2016) – https://tinyurl.com/y7wupzbc

Free online English audit – https://tinyurl.com/orenfwh

Free online maths audit – https://tinyurl.com/yatlyc55

Initial assessment for using technology – https://tinyurl.com/ztjfjuj

Online questionnaire – www.surveymonkey.com and www.smartsurvey.co.uk

Questionnaire design – https://tinyurl.com/mfqvc23

Reading list for the Minimum Core – https://tinyurl.com/y9shjcbj

Society for Education and Training (SET) – https://set.et-foundation.co.uk

# 6
# Professional development

## Introduction

This chapter will assist you in completing the fourth stage of your workbook by asking you to work through various activities.

It will explain how to partake in professional development, which is a vital part of your role, to ensure you remain current and competent as a teacher or a trainer.

It will also guide you in how to produce your development priorities and complete your professional development plan.

**This chapter will cover the following topics:**

- Summary of development priorities
- Professional development
- Professional development plan
- Continuing professional development activities

# Summary of development priorities

The summary of development priorities is the next section of the workbook which you can begin to complete when you are ready. It is based on the results of your self-assessment which you carried out as part of Chapter 5.

To meet the evidence requirements for QTLS status, your professional development must be current, i.e. carried out during the professional formation process. You will need to produce your priorities for your development and write these in the form of a summary.

Your summary should explain why you have decided to focus on a particular aspect of your practice, and the expected impact it will have on your learners. The content will be informed by the results of your self-assessment and your reflective comments, your first observation report and any other feedback received, such as that from your learners.

Your priorities should be in the form of *objectives*. They should include the areas you wish to develop, the action you will take, and what the expected impact will be. You will need to add completion dates for your objectives in each of the three areas of:

- teaching and learning (planning and delivery)
- teaching and learning (assessment)
- subject specialist knowledge.

The activities you choose to meet your objectives must be referenced to the Professional Standards (as in Appendix 1).

## *Activity*

*Access your workbook as before and go to the* Professional Development *section by clicking on the* Professional Development Plan *tab. Read the text on the screen. Now look at the Professional Standards (Appendix 1) and start thinking which ones you would like to develop which relate to each of the three areas in the bullet list above. You need to choose a minimum of one Professional Standard for each of the three areas.*

## Summary of development priorities

The summary of development priorities section in your workbook requires you to explain (in a maximum of 200 words) why you have decided to focus on particular aspects of your practice. If you look back at your combined results from the self-assessment tool (completed during the previous chapter and saved to your device as a PDF), you will be able to identify any areas that require development. Using the combined results will enable you to quickly identify key areas against the Professional Standards which require further development. You should look back at the document and read your reflective comments. This will help you to decide what action you should take and why.

## Activity

*Look back at your self-assessment report which will be under the Self-Assessment tab of your workbook. Scroll down and click on the v symbol, as in Figure 6.1, then click on the document title to open it.*

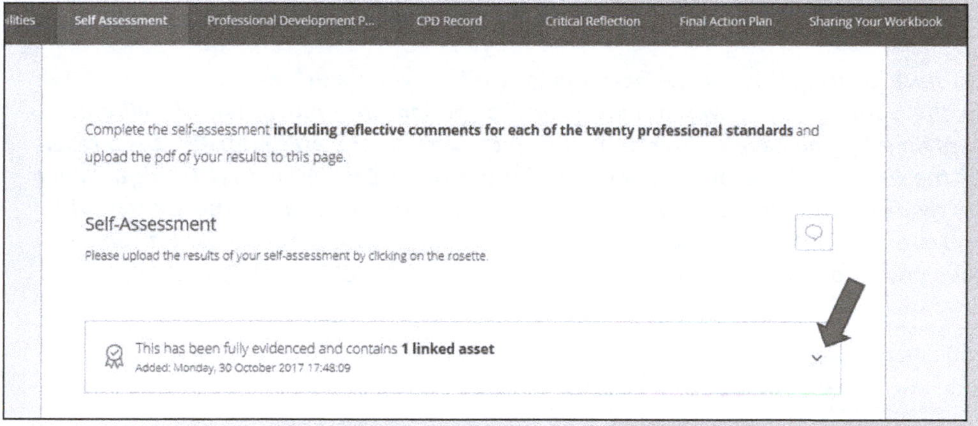

**Figure 6.1  Accessing your self-assessment report**

Information from your first observation report, your evaluation of the observation and learner feedback you have received can also be used to help create your objectives. You will need to identify key areas for improvement and key strengths. You could also consider the feedback you have received from other people, and think about any significant areas you wish to develop.

## Activity

*Look at your first observation report, your self-evaluation and learner and/or other feedback (from the Self-Assessment section of your workbook). Use these to help you list the key areas for your improvement, along with significant areas which you have identified for development.*

At this stage, you will find it helpful to arrange a meeting with your supporter. This will be to discuss the lists you have made and the actions you will take to meet your priorities (which should relate to the relevant Professional Standards you have chosen).

When you complete your development plan (explained later in this chapter), remember that you must have a minimum of one objective against each of the following three areas:

- teaching and learning (planning and delivery)

- teaching and learning (assessment)

- subject specialist knowledge.

## Activity

*Go back to the Professional Development tab in your workbook and scroll down to the Summary of Development Priorities section. In a maximum of 200 words, explain why you have chosen to focus on certain actions and priorities (as a result of the lists you have made). You could use a word processor first (or equivalent software) and then copy and paste your text into the box on the screen when you are ready. Add your text to your workbook, as in Figure 6.2. Don't forget to save your work and/or make a backup copy, if you haven't already done so.*

---

### Summary of Development Priorities

Tell us about the areas of your practice you intend to develop. Explain why you have decided to focus on these particular aspects of your practice, **informed by your self-assessment and first observation**. (Maximum 200 words).

I need to ensure my reflections are based on impact, are always learner focused, and systematically set myself challenging recorded targets to further improve my practice. I scored low on question 16 of the self-assessment. The first OTLA feedback endorses that I must be more confident in embedding and using every opportunity to develop maths and English in my lessons. I recognise that I lack confidence in my own ability, the BSKB will enable me to practise my skills, and peer observation will support my delivery in being creative and innovative, and improve my knowledge and understanding.

Undertaking peer observation will also support me to improve my planning around extension activities and homework tasks. I have booked on to an external CPD event called 'Supporting fair methods of assessment and providing valuable feedback'. I will also attend networking events and continue to engage in online forums such as LinkedIn and relevant Facebook groups. The professional discussion with my supporter was helpful in terms of identifying areas of good practice instead of focusing only on areas for development.

---

**Figure 6.2 Summary of Development Priorities (example)**

# Professional development

The professional development section of your workbook allows you to upload evidence in support of your summary of development priorities (which you have just keyed in). This could include, but is not limited to:

- notes from the meeting with your supporter (you can use the professional discussion template: *initial* section, which can be downloaded from your workbook)

- feedback from peers or colleagues

- a recent appraisal which refers to your professional development

- a recent action plan for your own development.

When you have your meeting with your supporter, you can use the professional discussion template to document it. You can download it by clicking on the link in the *Professional Development* section of your workbook. The *initial* section should be completed after you have had your meeting with your supporter to discuss your PDP. It's not mandatory to upload a copy of the template to your workbook; however, it helps to evidence the process.

You will need to complete your PDP, then have the professional discussion with your supporter, before coming back to the *Professional Development* section of your workbook to upload your evidence (by clicking on the red rosette). The next section of this chapter will explain how to create your PDP.

# Professional development plan

The professional development plan (PDP) is a mandatory part of the professional formation process and an essential tool for personal growth. It will support you in identifying your goals, required skills or a competency requirement you may have.

The text you have written as part of your professional development summary will help to inform your PDP. The plan relates to the three areas mentioned previously, which will need to be cross-referenced to the Professional Standards (as in Appendix 1).

To complete this section of your workbook, you will shortly need to add comments to the columns in the blank template on the screen (where it says *Enter text*). The first column asks you to state which of the Professional Standards you are referring to for each of the three areas:

- teaching and learning (planning and delivery)

- teaching and learning (assessment)

- subject specialist knowledge.

These three areas, with links to the Professional Standards and ideas for continuing professional development (CPD) activities will now be explained. Once you have read the following information, you will be able to start work on your PDP. There is a further section at the end of this chapter which gives more ideas for CPD activities.

## Teaching and learning: planning and delivery

Recommended Professional Standards (PS) for *planning and delivery* are:

- Planning and delivering to meet the diverse needs of learners (PS 1)

- Evaluate and challenge your practice, values and beliefs (PS 2)

- Inspire, motivate and raise aspirations of learners through your enthusiasm and knowledge (PS 3)

- Be creative and innovative in selecting and adapting strategies to help learners learn (PS 4)

- Value and promote social and cultural diversity, equality of opportunity and inclusion (PS5)

- Build positive and collaborative relationships with colleagues and learners (PS 6)

- Maintain and update your knowledge of educational research to develop evidence-based practice (PS 8)

- Apply theoretical understanding of effective practice in teaching, learning and assessment drawing on research and other evidence (PS 9)

- Manage and promote positive learner behaviour (PS 11)

- Understand the teaching and professional role and your responsibilities (PS 12)

- Plan and deliver effective learning programmes for diverse groups or individuals in a safe and inclusive environment (PS 14)

- Promote the benefits of technology and support learners in its use (PS 15)

- Address the mathematics and English needs of learners and work creatively to overcome individual barriers to learning (PS 16)

- Contribute to organisational development and quality improvement through collaboration with others (PS 20)

## Example

*Helen identified through her self-assessment evaluation that an area for her development was to better manage learner behaviour. This was also supported by her observation report, where an area for development was to promote positive learner behaviour. Therefore, Helen decided under* Teaching and learning: planning and delivery *to focus on Professional Standard number 11:* Manage and promote positive learner behaviour.

*Example CPD activities for Teaching and learning: planning and delivery*

Activities you could undertake to meet this area include the following. You will only need to carry out and evidence one, which could be something other than those listed here:

- addressing the maths and English needs of learners and working creatively to overcome individual barriers to learning

- using creative and innovative ways to help learners to learn

- increasing the use of technology in your role and promoting its use to your learners

- inspiring, motivating and raising the aspirations of your learners

- managing and promoting positive learner behaviour

- observing a peer to share effective practice in using technology

- planning and delivering effective learning programmes for diverse groups or individuals in a safe and inclusive environment

- reading research articles on strategies to improve behaviour management and testing ideas out in practice

- self-assessing your maths and/or English skills and undertaking some online modules to develop your skills. Taking a practice test to demonstrate progress

- using strategies/methods to demonstrate that you value and promote social and cultural diversity, equality of opportunity and inclusion

- updating your own maths and English skills to ensure you have the confidence to support your learners to improve these skills.

## Tip

*There are some free online learning programmes for members of the Society for Education and Training (SET) at this link:*

*https://tinyurl.com/y8b8hx7w. You will need to create an account and log in.*

# Teaching and Learning: assessment

Recommended Professional Standards for *assessment* are:

- Planning and delivering to meet the diverse needs of learners (PS 1)

- Build positive and collaborative relationships with colleagues and learners (PS 6)

- Maintain and update your knowledge of educational research to develop evidence-based practice (PS 8)

- Apply theoretical understanding of effective practice in teaching, learning and assessment drawing on research and other evidence (PS 9)

- Understand the teaching and professional role and your responsibilities (PS 12)

- Motivate and inspire learners to promote achievement and develop their skills to enable progression (PS 13)

- Enable learners to share responsibility for their own learning and assessment, setting goals that stretch and challenge (PS 17)

- Apply appropriate and fair methods of assessment and provide constructive and timely feedback to support progression and achievement (PS 18)

- Contribute to organisational development and quality improvement through collaboration with others (PS 20)

## Example

*Havid identified through his self-assessment that learners did not take much responsibility for their own learning. His observation report had recommended that he should start to use peer-assessment to stretch and challenge individuals. Therefore, Havid decided under* Teaching and learning: assessment *to focus on* Professional Standard 17: **Enable learners to share responsibility for their own learning and assessment, setting goals that stretch and challenge.**

*Example CPD activities for Teaching and Learning: assessment*

Activities you could undertake to meet this area include the following. You will only need to carry out and evidence one, which could be something other than those listed here:

- applying appropriate and fair methods of assessment and providing constructive and timely feedback to support progression and achievement

- collaborating with an English teacher in order to develop skills in providing constructive written feedback to learners on their English skills

- enabling learners to share responsibility for their own learning and assessment, setting goals that stretch and challenge

- motivating and inspiring learners to promote achievement and developing their skills to enable progression, taking into account their individual needs

- undertaking peer observations to develop skills in stretching learners of all abilities and testing out in practice

- reading of educational theory on formative assessment strategies and testing out and evaluation of impact on practice and learners.

## Tip

*There are some free resources and lots of information to help with your CPD at this link: https://tinyurl.com/y7ermcan*

## Subject specialist knowledge

Recommended Professional Standards for *subject specialist knowledge* are:

- Build positive and collaborative relationships with colleagues and learners (PS 6)

- Maintain and update knowledge of your subject and/or vocational area (PS 7)

- Maintain and update your knowledge of educational research to develop evidence-based practice (PS 8)

- Evaluate your practice with others and assess its impact on learning (PS 10)

- Maintain and update your teaching and training expertise and vocational skills through collaboration with employers (PS 19)

- Contribute to organisational development and quality improvement through collaboration with others (PS 20)

## Example

*Karolina identified through the self-assessment process that, although she made links to employability during her delivery, she had not worked in industry for over three years. She felt she lacked the most up-to-date skills and knowledge. Karolina also thought it would be beneficial for her learners to have guest speakers direct from industry to discuss the benefits and challenges of working in her specialist subject area. Therefore, Karolina decided under* **Subject specialist knowledge** *to focus on Professional Standard 19:* **Maintain and update your teaching and training expertise and vocational skills through collaboration with employers.**

*Example CPD activities for subject specialist knowledge*

Activities you could undertake to meet this area include the following. You will only need to carry out and evidence one, which could be something other than those listed here:

- attending courses/updates related to your subject specialism during the process of professional formation

- co-designing and co-delivering programmers with employer partners (including apprenticeships)

- collaborating with colleagues to expand your knowledge and understanding of your subject/vocational area

- keeping yourself updated on your subject/vocational area so that your learners receive the benefit of the latest knowledge and skills

- maintaining and updating your teaching and training expertise and vocational skills through collaboration with others outside your organisation, e.g. through links with employers, occupational networking, trade and professional memberships, links with the wider community, presenting at a conference

- undertaking peer observations of colleagues and putting into practice something learnt from the observation and evaluating its impact on learners

- revising the curriculum/programme content after talking to/visiting employers

- visiting an employer or undertaking a placement in industry

- working part time or undertaking a placement in your subject/occupational area.

---

### Tip

*Always keep records of the CPD activities you undertake, not just those you are doing to gain QTLS status. Records of CPD are often asked for by inspectors and quality assurers.*

---

Now that you are familiar with examples of CPD to meet the three areas and the Professional Standards, you can begin to consider your objectives, i.e. the activities you will undertake.

## SMART targets

It's always beneficial to use SMART targets when planning the activities you will undertake. These will enable you to focus on what needs to be done effectively and within the expected completion dates. Your targets (the objectives you have set yourself) should be challenging enough to ensure your development is progressive, yet have a positive impact on your learners.

SMART stands for:

**S**pecific – are the targets clearly defined to the three areas (planning and development; assessment for learning; and subject specialist knowledge) and clearly referenced to the Professional Standards?

**M**easurable – how will you know the activity undertaken has had an impact? What are you looking for which proves it?

**A**chievable – are the activities possible? Who else will need to be involved?

**R**elevant – is the activity appropriate? Is it going to have the expected impact or outcome? Who will it benefit and why?

**T**ime bound – are the dates achievable within the professional formation process deadlines?

## Example

*Morgan teaches a group of Entry Level 2 learners. He has identified through the self-assessment process and through a recent observation report that his planning and delivery does not embrace British Values. He has also recognised that some of his learners' behaviour demonstrates a lack of respect for others. He therefore identifies Professional Standard number 5:* Value and promote social and cultural diversity, equality of opportunity and inclusion *would support him in addressing the learners' needs. Table 6.1 is an example of how he has written his SMART targets.*

### Table 6.1 Example SMART targets

| Professional Standard and specific areas for development | Activity to be undertaken | Anticipated impact on learners | Expected date this will be achieved |
|---|---|---|---|
| Planning and Delivery (PS 5)<br><br>Learners will list a minimum of three British Values and demonstrate a minimum of two | Revisit scheme of work and lesson plan to embed British Values in my delivery through activities for the duration of the course<br><br>Support learners in identifying when they are demonstrating the British Values | 100% of learners will list a minimum of three British Values and demonstrate a minimum of two | February 20** |

When writing your targets, try not to use the words *know, learn,* or *understand.* These are not SMART and you would find it difficult to measure what development has actually taken place.

## Activity

*Consider which Professional Standards you wish to develop, and which of the three areas they relate to:*

- *teaching and learning (planning and delivery)*
- *teaching and learning (assessment)*
- *subject specialist knowledge.*

*Write an objective for each of the above, and cross reference them to a relevant Professional Standard. Remember that they should be based on the results of your self-assessment and supporting documents. Consider what CPD you will do to meet them, the anticipated impact on your learners and a date when you expect to complete by.*

*Add this information to the Professional Development Plan on the screen, as in Figure 6.3.*

*Once you have keyed in a line of text, you will see a* ⊠ *symbol to the right of each line. Only click on it if you wish to delete the whole line, for example, if you have changed your mind about something after the discussion with your supporter.*

| Responsibilities | Self Assessment | **Professional Development...** | CPD Record | Critical Reflection | Final Action Plan |
| --- | --- | --- | --- | --- | --- |

### Professional Development Plan

Please complete the Professional Development Plan below

| Professional Standard and specific area for development | Activity to be undertaken (e.g. meeting with colleagues, peer observation, CPD event, visit to employer, research or professional reading) | Anticipated impact on learners (e.g. what difference will the outcomes of this action make to your learners?) | Expected date this will be completed by |
| --- | --- | --- | --- |
| *Enter text...* | *Enter text...* | *Enter text...* | *Enter text...* |

**Figure 6.3 Template – Professional Development Plan**

Now that you have created your PDP, you can share it with your supporter and arrange to have a professional discussion with them. You can share it by clicking on the *I want to* button at the top right of the page. Make sure you have a copy of the Professional Discussion template (click on the link in the Professional Discussion section of your workbook). Your supporter might give you some valuable advice, therefore you can return to the template on the screen and change what you have keyed in should you wish to.

*Partake in the professional discussion with your supporter to discuss your PDP. Complete the template and save it to your device. Return to the* Professional Development *section of your workbook to upload it, along with any other relevant evidence (by clicking on the red rosette). You might wish to update your PDP at this stage if relevant. You can add text to the box if you wish, and then choose* This item is now fully evidenced.

*Tick the box at the end of the page to* Mark page as complete *(once you are sure it is all completed).*

# Continuing professional development activities

Continuing professional development can be anything that you do which helps you to improve your practice and keep current with your subject knowledge. Undertaking CPD is a vital part of being an exceptional practitioner. It enables you to stay up to date with your specialist subject, including any changes, and new and emerging technologies. CPD supports you to remain *industry ready*, i.e. *current*, regarding knowledge which relates to the subject you teach. This will have a positive impact on your learners, as you will be able to prepare them for the world of work. In addition, CPD activities enable you to remain current in terms of teaching, learning and assessment approaches. Gaining an initial teacher education qualification is just the start of your journey; undertaking the right CPD activities is what makes you an exceptional practitioner in the long term.

*There are CPD modules available as part of Foundation Online Learning (FOL) and the Excellence Gateway, which are mapped to the Professional Standards. They are based on many subject areas and you might find them useful for your development. You can access them here: https://tinyurl.com/CPDFOLEG*

As part of the professional formation process, you will have identified an objective for each of the following areas:

- teaching and learning (planning and delivery)
- teaching and learning (assessment)
- subject specialist knowledge.

This means you will carry out at least three different CPD activities which you will have cross-referenced to the Professional Standards.

Examples of CPD activities can include:

- attending a conference

- attending a seminar

- attending an event

- challenging own practice

- coaching and mentoring

- employer visit

- engaging with a new group

- partaking in a discussion

- reading, e.g. educational research/theory

- representing your department/college

- sharing practice with peers

- training delivery/cascading

- undertaking a peer observation

- undertaking an action research project

- using new technology.

- working towards a course (online, face to face, blended).

## Activity

*Take a look at the Example activities for your CPD at the following link to gain further ideas for your CPD: https://tinyurl.com/y7kwjp75*

Prior to planning or undertaking any CPD, you might like to ask yourself the following questions:

- Why am I doing it and what will I gain as a result?

- What will be the impact on me, my learners and the organisation?

- Is it really relevant and/or necessary that I do it?

- Is there any funding available for me to undertake CPD?

- How much of my own time and/or money will I need to invest?

- How can I apply the CPD I have done to my practice?

- Can I share it with others; if so, who and why?

- Who can support me and give me advice whilst I undertake it?

- What will the role of my manager/mentor be?

- Are there any organisational implications as a result of my undertaking CPD?

- When is the best time to review my progress, and update my action plan and CPD record?

You might think of a few more questions besides those listed. The important point is that all CPD should have an impact, not just be something that you do because you think you should, or because someone tells you to.

## Activity

*Carry out the CPD activities which you have planned. You will need to have completed them prior to moving onto the next section of your workbook. You may find the* QTLS Professional Standards Research Map *and the* Online research library *(see Chapter 7) will prove useful to help evidence your CPD activities.*

When you reach the critical reflection section of your workbook (covered in Chapter 8), you must comment on how your reading of relevant theory and research has influenced your development. You might like to start thinking now about books, journals and online articles which could help you with your CPD.

# Summary

This chapter has explored how to complete the fourth stage of your workbook. This included how to partake in professional development, how to write your development priorities and complete your professional development plan.

You might like to carry out further research by accessing the books and websites listed at the end of this chapter.

This chapter has covered the following topics:

- Summary of development priorities

- Professional development

- Professional development plan

- Continuing professional development activities

# References and further information

Friedman, A. (2012) *Continuing Professional Development*. London: Routledge.

Neary, S. (2016) *CPD for the Career Development Professional: A Handbook for Enhancing Practice*. Bath: Trotman.

Scales, P., Pickering, J., Senior, L., Headley, K., Garner, P. and Boulton, H. (2011) *Continuing Professional Development in the Lifelong Learning Sector*. Maidenhead: OU Press.

# Websites

Ann Gravells: CPD information – https://tinyurl.com/n6tbs68

Society for Education and Training (SET): Webinars – https://tinyurl.com/SETwebinars

# 7

# Continuing professional development record

---

**Introduction**

This chapter will assist you in completing the fifth stage of your workbook by asking you to work through various activities.

It will explain how to use and negotiate the QTLS Professional Standards Research Map as well as the online research library, to gain information and knowledge to evidence your continuing professional development (CPD).

It will also guide you how to record your CPD, and explain how to partake in the interim professional discussion with your supporter.

**This chapter will cover the following topics:**

- QTLS Professional Standards Research Map
- Online research library
- Continuing professional development record
- Professional discussion – interim

---

# QTLS Professional Standards Research Map

To be able to complete your CPD record for the next stage of your workbook, you will need to have carried out the CPD activities which you identified as part of your professional development plan in Chapter 6.

The QTLS Professional Standards Research Map and the Online research library (covered in the next section of this chapter) include useful information and activities which you can undertake to help evidence your CPD. They will prove particularly useful at directing you to relevant theory and research, which you must study and carry out as part of your CPD. You will be required to comment on how your reading and research has impacted upon your practice, as part of the critical reflection section of your workbook (covered in Chapter 8).

The Society for Education and Training (SET) has produced a Professional Standards Research Map (also known as the *QTLS Interactive Map*), as in Figure 7.1. It is a tool designed to give you quick and straightforward access to a good selection of resources, such as information and knowledge, which is drawn from relevant research. It does this by aligning the resources to the Professional Standards and by offering a range of materials for you to access. These range from short, bite-sized summaries to more in-depth research reports.

**Figure 7.1 QTLS Professional Standards Research Map**

## Activity

*Take a look at the QTLS Professional Standards Research Map at this link: https:// tinyurl.com/ycx93mw5*

*Click on the symbol above the words* Start here – How to use the QTLS Professional Standards Research Map *(top left) and read the information leaflet which appears in a new window. You can save this document if you wish by right clicking on it and choosing* Save as.

*Close the instructions window and you will return to the map. You can then click on any of the symbols above the 20 Professional Standards to access further information and relevant links to materials and resources.*

You might find that, when using the QTLS Professional Standards Research Map, further information opens in new windows or tabs. If so, you will need to click back on to the original window or tab to return to the QTLS Professional Standards Research Map. The information and materials you access will be useful to support your CPD. You could make notes of how you have used the resources, how they relate to the Professional Standards and what impact they have had, to help evidence your CPD.

## Tip

*You can use the QTLS Professional Standards Research Map at any point during your professional formation process to help improve your knowledge. You can also access it again at any point in your future career to help maintain your CPD.*

To gain QTLS status, you will need to be able to demonstrate how you are continuing to develop your teaching skills as well as your subject specialist knowledge. This is all part of being a dual professional. Some of your knowledge will be drawn from your own research and from other formal evidence. It is a mandatory requirement to provide evidence of pro-fessional reading which you have undertaken, which has informed improvements in your practice. There are opportunities to refer to this as part of your CPD record and as part of your critical reflection (covered in Chapter 8). The map will therefore help you with your research and reading.

# Online research library

SET members can access an online research library which is powered by EBSCO Information Services. EBSCO is an acronym for **E**lton **B**. **S**tephens **Co**. It began in 1944 and is a division of EBSCO Industries Inc., which is a family-owned company in the USA.

Accessing journals, videos and other sources of information is a great way of maintaining your CPD. When you do, don't forget to make notes of how you have used the resources in relation to the Professional Standards.

The research library and journal collection comprises a wide range of national and international education research allowing you to deepen your teaching and training expertise.

For example, there are online links to:

- TED Talks/Videos

- Browse all eBooks

- Browse Video Collection

- Browse all Audio Summaries

- Harvard Business School Press

- Browse all Business Book Summaries

- Center for Creative Leadership Videos.

As a member of SET, you can gain access to articles from more than 1,300 education journals, 530 eBooks and monographs, and 2,300 education-related conference papers.

In addition, EBSCO's specially curated selection of articles on teaching leadership, career development and personal development will provide the latest advice and information to help you develop your employability and management skills.

## Activity

*Log into your account on SET's website and access the online library at this link: https://tinyurl.com/y856dkhe. You can browse by themes or just key in a topic in the search box to see what's available.*

There is also a link to access TED talks. TED is a non-profit organisation devoted to spreading ideas, usually in the form of videos of short, powerful talks (18 minutes or less). TED began in 1984 as a conference where Technology, Entertainment and Design converged (hence the acronym TED) and today covers almost all topics from science to business to global issues, in more than 100 languages.

## Tip

*You can access the TED talks without being a member of SET at https://www.ted. com/*

# Continuing professional development record

To help you keep track of the activities you undertake, you will need to complete a CPD record. It is designed to enable you to keep track of what you have done, and to provide evidence of your development. A template is provided which you can download and use.

## Activity

*Access your workbook as before, and click on the CPD Record tab. Read the text on the screen. Click on the link as in Figure 7.2 and download the CPD record template (you will need to scroll down the list of documents which opens up in a new window, until you see My QTLS, then look for CPD Record and click on it). Save the template to your computer or device.*

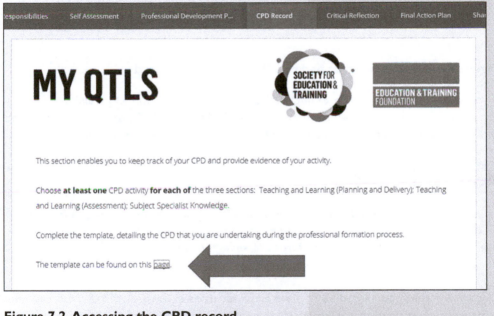

**Figure 7.2 Accessing the CPD record**

When you completed your professional development plan (PDP) as part of Chapter 6, you will have planned a minimum of one objective (or CPD activity) against each of the following three areas:

- teaching and learning (planning and delivery)
- teaching and learning (assessment)
- subject specialist knowledge.

You might have carried out several CPD activities for each area. There is no maximum, as long as what you have done is relevant and meets the Professional Standards. Some of your activities will be evidenced as documents, for example, a peer observation. Others can be your written notes regarding reading and research which you have undertaken.

When documenting the CPD activities you have carried out, you will need to log them against the three areas (see the columns in Figure 7.3), as well as cross-referencing them to the Professional Standards by adding an X in the relevant column. You can include the relevant Professional Standard (PS) number in brackets, e.g. (PS 2).

| Activity Date (s) and Duration | Activity Description | Put an 'X' in the professional standard area(s) below that apply (ies) to your CPD activity | | | Link to Supporting Evidence |
| --- | --- | --- | --- | --- | --- |
| | | 1) Teaching and Learning: Planning and Delivery (e.g. standards 1, 2, 3, 4, 5, 6, 8, 9, 11, 12, 14, 15, 16, 20) | 2) Teaching and Learning: Assessment (e.g. standards 1, 6, 8, 9, 12, 13, 17, 18, 20) | 3) Subject Specialist knowledge (e.g. standards 6, 7, 8, 10, 19, 20) | |
| 04/12 (3hrs) 22/12 (2hrs) 07/02 (1hr) 07/02 (1hr) | • Peer Observation • Professional discussion (interim) • 2nd Observation of teaching learning and assessment • Evaluation from above OTLA | X (PS 2) | | | • Professional Discussion (interim) • OTLA report • Evaluation • Reflection 2 |

**Figure 7.3 CPD record mapped to a Professional Standard**

If you would like to see more examples, the Society for Education and Training (SET) has produced two case studies which show extracts of CPD records. These can be accessed at the following links: https://tinyurl.com/yb498ejz and https://tinyurl.com/yb4ul683

## Activity

*Using the CPD record which you downloaded to your computer or device, key in the details of your activities and cross-reference them to the Professional Standards, as in Figure 7.3. Don't forget to save your document.*

Once you have documented all of your CPD activities in each of the three areas, and cross-referenced them to the Professional Standards, you will need to upload your CPD record and supporting evidence to your workbook. The evidence is the proof that you have carried out the CPD activities. Make sure you have saved the files beforehand, and that you know where to access them.

## Activity

*Scroll down to the CPD Record section of your workbook. Upload your completed CPD record and supporting evidence to your workbook by clicking on the red rosette. Click on Add additional asset to add more documents. You can add text to the box if you wish, and then choose This item is now fully evidenced.*

# Professional discussion – interim

The professional discussion is the next section of your workbook on the *CPD Record* page.

A professional discussion is an opportunity to have a conversation with your supporter about your progress so far. It gives you the opportunity to justify what you have achieved, and to gain advice and support.

SET guidance suggests three professional discussions between yourself and your supporter:

1. initial

2. interim

3. final.

Only one is mandatory, which relates to your CPD and is known as the *interim* professional discussion. The others are *initial* (which you might have completed as part of the Professional Development Plan section of your workbook in the previous chapter) and the *final* professional discussion (which can be completed during the Final Action Plan section of your workbook, as in Chapter 9). Don't worry if you haven't carried out the *initial* discussion, as long as you partake in the *interim* discussion and provide evidence of it, you will be fine.

Prior to the interim professional discussion taking place, you should agree a date and time with your supporter, along with the nature of the content of the discussion. This will enable you to prepare in advance, and you will find it useful to have a copy of the Professional Standards to refer to (see Appendix 1). You may need to bring along examples of teaching materials or professional development activities which you have documented in your CPD record. This will enable you to discuss them with your supporter.

You can access the professional discussion template in advance via your workbook, as in Figure 7.4. It is in three sections: *initial*; *interim*; and *final*. It must be completed after each discussion and signed by you and your supporter. The only mandatory discussion you must partake in relates to the *interim* section of the template. However, it is good practice to have regular discussions with your supporter and you might like to have *initial* and *final* discussions, as well as the mandatory *interim* discussion.

## 2) Professional Discussion

Please upload your **signed and dated** notes from the professional discussion with your supporter or colleague regarding a review of your progress in relation to your professional development plan.

You can use the template here. Click on the rosette to upload the notes.

Remember, you can share your workbook at anytime with your supporter by going to your assets folder, click once on your workbook from the list, then click on the Share button and select your supporter's name from the contacts list.

**Figure 7.4 Accessing the professional discussion template**

*Go to the* CPD Record *tab of your workbook and scroll down to the* Professional Discussion *section. Download the professional discussion template and save it to your computer or device ready for use later (if you haven't previously done this).*

## Partaking in the professional discussion

The professional discussion should ideally be in a quiet area where you and your supporter will not be disturbed. It usually takes about 40 minutes to one hour, and notes can be added to the template. You and your supporter will need to agree who is going to be responsible for making the notes and who will complete the template. You could make a digital audio recording of the discussion to refer to, if you would rather not make notes at the time. The recording could be uploaded to your workbook, if you wish, as evidence.

Ideally, the professional discussion should take place face to face, as your supporter will probably be working in the same organisation as yourself. However, if that is not possible, then it can be carried out virtually, i.e. by using Skype or via a smart phone.

When you are taking part in the professional discussion, remember to remain focused; don't digress, but be specific with your responses to the questions you are asked, and give clear examples of what you have achieved.

*Arrange a date and time with your supporter for the* interim *professional discussion.*

The interim professional discussion should be based on the CPD activities you have undertaken to date. It should relate to the impact of those activities in relation to your professional practice, your learners and your organisation, and how they link to the Professional Standards. Any CPD activities not yet completed can be addressed in your final professional discussion, which will be explained in Chapter 9.

At the end of the discussion, your supporter should confirm what you have achieved and whether there is anything you still need to do, and, if so, when you should achieve it by. Both you and your supporter should sign the template to authenticate the document. You can then scan the document to your computer or device, before uploading it to your workbook.

*Partake in the professional discussion with your supporter and complete the relevant page as per your conversation, ensure it is signed and dated. Scan or take a photo of it and save it to your computer or device. Scroll down to the* **Professional Discussion** *section of your workbook and upload it by clicking on the red rosette. You can add text to the box if you wish, and then choose* **This item is now fully evidenced.**

*Tick the box at the end of the page to* **Mark page as complete** *(once you are sure it is all completed).*

# Summary

This chapter has explored how to complete the fifth stage of your workbook. This included the different ways to record your CPD and how to take part in the interim professional discussion. How to use and negotiate the QTLS Professional Standards Research Map has also been covered.

This chapter has covered the following topics:

- QTLS Professional Standards Research Map

- Online research library

- Continuing professional development record

- Professional discussion – interim

You might like to carry out further research by accessing the books and websites listed at the end of this chapter.

# References and further information

Friedman, A. (2012) *Continuing Professional Development.* Abingdon: Routledge.

Megginson, D. (2007) *Continuing Professional Development.* London: Kogan Page.

Scales, P., Pickering, J., Senior, L., Headley, K., Garner, P. and Boulton, H. (2011) *Continuing Professional Development in the Lifelong Learning Sector.* Maidenhead: OU Press.

# Websites

Brilliant Teaching and Training in FE and Skills: A Guide to Effective CPD for Teachers, Trainers and Leaders – http://tinyurl.com/ocsef6o

EBSCO – https://www.ebsco.com/

Excellence Gateway: Improving Teaching – https://tinyurl.com/ycfdmcx9

Guidelines for CPD – https://tinyurl.com/os92nqe

Review of CPD – https://tinyurl.com/os92nqe

Reading list for reflection and CPD, Ann Gravells – https://tinyurl.com/y9q9eh5j

Ofsted Teaching, Learning and Assessment in Further Education and Skills – What Works and Why (2014) – http://tinyurl.com/pf52qlx

Society for Education and Training (SET) – CPD resources https://tinyurl.com/y92lxqn2

TED talks – https://www.ted.com/

# 8

# Critical reflection

## Introduction

This chapter will assist you in completing the sixth stage of your workbook by asking you to work through various activities.

It will help you to explore the positive impact of undertaking the professional formation process by carrying out a process of critical reflection. It will guide you to provide an informed reflective account of the professional development activities you have undertaken.

It will also guide you how to evaluate the impact your activities have had on your post-14 practice, your learners and your organisation.

**This chapter will cover the following topics:**

- Reflective account
- Evidence for improvements in post-14 practice
- Evidence of the impact on learner outcomes
- Evidence of the impact of your professional formation on your organisation

# Reflective account

The reflective account is part of the *Critical Reflection* section of the workbook which you can begin to complete when you are ready. It requires you to look back at the professional development activities which you have undertaken throughout the whole professional formation process, and to reflect upon your practice.

You will need to critically reflect regarding the impact of your professional development on:

- improvements in post-14 practice with learners
- the outcomes of your learners (i.e. their achievements)
- your organisation.

You should also consider the impact upon your peers and colleagues.

## What is reflective practice?

Reflection means taking a step back, looking at your own practice and identifying something that is happening or has happened. It could be something you have done well or something you think could have gone better. Imagine you are watching another teacher with their learners, you might ask:

- How was their performance?
- How much learning actually took place, and what was the impact of this learning upon the learners?
- What could be done differently and why?
- What could change and why?

Asking these questions about your own practice can help you become more reflective. You can do this after every lesson you teach, not just the ones for the professional formation process.

To help you carry out an informed reflection of your practice, you could look back at your evidence, such as the observation report, and learner and peer feedback, to inform your thoughts. This will help you to identify areas to improve and develop. Be really honest with yourself; reflection is not about being annoyed with yourself, it's about recognising your own development needs in order to improve your practice. This could be a strength to be further developed, or a weakness that needs addressing. The main consideration should always be about the impact, i.e. what will the impact be if you develop, change or improve something? Will it be positive for your learners, your colleagues and/or your organisation? If not, why not?

*Critical evaluation*

The reflective account section of your workbook asks you to *critically evaluate*. Being *critical* is about using *skilful judgement* when reflecting on the impact that the professional formation process has had upon your practice. To *evaluate* that impact is to *judge the significance* of it.

The following are examples of teachers critically evaluating their practice, which have been cross-referenced to the Professional Standards (PS) as in Appendix 1.

## Example 1

*After undertaking the self-assessment and receiving feedback from his first observation, Steven recognised he tended to blame the learners for turning up late to his class or not attending at all, rather than looking at himself. As part of his professional development, Steven has developed classroom strategies to stretch and challenge all individuals. These have included frequent changes of activities. In the past six weeks there has been no instance of learners arriving late to class, and attendance has improved by 86 per cent. (PS 1, 2, 3, 4)*

Steven has reflected upon the results of his self-assessment and feedback from his first observation. He has been critical by making a skilful judgement regarding the fact that he was blaming his learners rather than himself. He has evaluated the situation by accepting he needs to change. The significance of this is that there has been a positive impact on his learners' arrival times and attendance.

## Example 2

*As part of her professional development, Emma has researched World Skills competitions for her vocational area. She has also delivered in-house competitions for her learners to decide who will represent the class at a local level. The learner surveys identified all learners felt they have improved their employability skills as a result of the competition activities. This was an area Emma wanted to develop, to improve her self-assessment score for Professional Standard 13.*

*Emma has shared the information with her colleagues to enable them to prepare their own learners for inclusion in the competitions. This has not only had a positive impact on Emma's learners, but also on the whole organisation. Most of the learners have engaged in the employer-led competitions and the local media are now following the story. (PS 6, 13, 17, 19, 20)*

Emma has reflected upon the results of her self-assessment and has addressed Professional Standard 13. She has been critical by making a skilful judgement to identify other professional standards she could strengthen to benefit herself, her organisation, her colleagues and learners.

Aspects to help you become more critical can include:

- asking yourself if you have changed your delivery and/or assessment style based on:
  - o the results of learner surveys and/or learner feedback
  - o feedback from the observations of your teaching, learning and assessment practice
  - o feedback from peer observations
  - o advice from colleagues

- looking back at the professional discussion records with your supporter (or other relevant person) and considering what you have learnt about yourself as a practitioner

- analysing data and statistics such as enrolment, retention, achievement, destinations and progression

- looking for trends or patterns to find out why things are occurring.

You can also consider what information, knowledge and materials you have found helpful from using the QTLS Professional Standards Research Map (as in Chapter 7), and how you used it to improve your own knowledge and performance. For example, you may have shared aspects with colleagues which resulted in an improvement to their working practice, and to your organisation as a whole.

## Activity

*Look back at your self-assessment notes and your professional development plan (PDP). If you don't have them saved on your device, log in to* My QTLS *and click on the* Self-Assessment *tab to view your self-assessment notes, then the* Professional Development *tab to view your PDP. Consider what you are doing differently now, compared to what you were doing prior to your self-assessment. You might like to make some notes to help you critically evaluate what you have done and what you have learnt. These notes will be useful for your reflective account.*

## Writing your reflective account

To help you write your reflective account, the Society for Education and Training (SET) suggests using three questions.

*Question 1*

*Look back at your self-assessment and professional development plan. Reflect on how you have addressed the professional standards you identified in your development plan. Critically evaluate the impact the process has had on your learners. How has any reading you identified developed your understanding of your practice?*

To achieve this, you can start by making notes based on the following:

- referring to the Professional Standards (see Appendix 1) and reflecting on how you have addressed them

- looking at your self-assessment results and reviewing your professional development plan to see how you have improved

- critically evaluating the impact upon your learners, for example:

  o improvements in attendance, retention and achievement rates

  o a better classroom atmosphere, i.e. the learners are more settled and more confident to ask questions

  o learner behaviour, motivation and morale have improved

  o learners are arriving to class on time (or early) and are more willing to collaborate with each other

  o learners are fully engaging in the learning process and taking responsibility for their own learning

- considering examples of how you have developed your practice based upon the reading you have carried out, perhaps as a result of using the QTLS Professional Standards Research Map.

## Tip

*You can use the self-assessment tool and carry out the self-assessment process again to give you a measure of your progress. It can be accessed at this link: https://tinyurl.com/hms9x92. You will be able to save and print a copy if you wish.*

*Question 2*

*What has been the impact on your colleagues and your organisation and how do discussions with peers support your ongoing development?*

To achieve this, you can start by making notes based on the following:

- referring to the Professional Standards (see Appendix 1) and reflecting on how you have addressed them

- how collaborating with colleagues has helped improve their knowledge and skills, i.e. the sharing of good practice to enable them to try different delivery and/or assessment approaches

- how greater cross-curriculum and/or departmental working has showed signs of improvement

- how you have fostered and/or developed and strengthened external links with other providers, employers, higher education establishments and/or other agencies to improve communication for all concerned

- how you have helped create a community of research and practice amongst colleagues to enable a standardised approach to learning, and to improve learner support.

## Tip

*You should continue to collaborate and share best practice with your colleagues after the professional formation process has finished.*

Question 3

*How have your professional values, professional knowledge and skills developed during the process? What have you learnt about yourself as a practitioner?*

To achieve this, you can start by making notes based on the following:

- referring to the Professional Standards (see Appendix 1) and reflecting on how you have addressed them

- how you have improved the way you embed equality and diversity during your lessons to develop your own values and those of your learners

- how you have overcome a fear, for example, by taking a course to improve your numeracy/maths skills

- looking back at the feedback from the observations of your practice. Some organisations still grade observations and there may have been an improvement in your grade from one observation to the next. What do you think the reason for this is? If your organisation doesn't give grades after an observation, has there been an improvement in the feedback you have received and, if so, why do you think this is?

- reviewing specific examples of creative and innovative approaches to teaching, learning and assessment and the impact this has had on your practice, for example, how using new technology has improved your confidence to try new approaches with your learners

- testing out new ideas which have been based on the reading and research you have undertaken, and how this has impacted in a positive way upon your practice

- stating what you have learnt about yourself as a practitioner, for example, how your communication skills have improved; how your planning, delivery and assessment skills have improved; how your knowledge of your subject has improved.

## Tip

*You should refer to the Professional Standards continually throughout your career, to ensure you are developing your practice in relation to meeting them (as in Appendix 1).*

Once you have made notes relating to the three questions, you will need to check that you have critically evaluated the impact upon your learners, your colleagues, your organisation and yourself. You will need to write your account clearly and within 1,500 words. You don't need to refer to theories or theorists.

As this is a long piece of writing, if you haven't keyed in your work to a word processor first, and saved it, you might like to copy and paste it from your workbook into a document. You would not want to lose all your text at this point. If you can't do this, make sure you save your workbook regularly by clicking on Save in the top left corner of the screen.

## Activity

*Click the Critical Reflection tab at the top of your workbook and scroll down until you see Reflective Account. Read the text on the page (which relates to the three questions).*

*In a maximum of 1,500 words, key into the box an informed reflective account of the professional development activities you have undertaken during the whole process of your professional formation. You can do this by addressing the three questions. Critically evaluate the effect which each has had on your post-14 practice, the outcomes of your learners and your organisation. You could use a word processor first (or equivalent software) and then copy and paste your text into the box on the screen when you are ready. Don't forget to save your work.*

# Evidence for improvements in post-14 practice

You will need to demonstrate that you have made improvements to your practice throughout the professional formation process. Post-14 practice means working with learners aged 14 plus (i.e. in years 10, 11 and above) and/or with adults. Your practice for the purpose of professional formation should include working with groups, not just working with individuals on a one-to-one basis.

You will need to upload various pieces of evidence to your workbook to support your reflective account and you will need to have had your second observation by this point.

## Activity

*If you haven't had your second observation yet, arrange for this to take place with your supporter. It should be at least three months after your first observation. Partake in the observation when you are ready and make sure you obtain a signed and dated copy of the observation report.*

Evidence for this section includes:

- observation of teaching, learning and assessment (OTLA) report: final. This can be carried out by a manager, a colleague, a mentor or your supporter and will be documented on your organisation's own observation form. It must demonstrate the impact of your professional development plan (as explained in Chapter 6). The report must be signed and dated, and completed during the final month before submitting your workbook. This final observation should be at least three months after your first observation

- your lesson plan for the final observation

- your self-evaluation regarding the observed lesson. This must include reference to learner feedback you have received. SET does not provide a template for this, you can use your organisation's or design your own.

Other evidence (which is not mandatory) includes:

- learner feedback forms regarding the observed lesson, which support your self-evaluation comments (remove any names to ensure confidentiality)

- your scheme of work which you used for the group of learners you were observed with during the professional formation process. This can be annotated to show the particular lesson that was observed.

If you are teaching in a one-to-one setting, it is possible to use evidence from this, but you must be able to produce evidence of at least one observation which has been carried out in a group teaching context (five learners or more).

If you are unable to be observed in this timescale, or feel you cannot meet all the evidence requirements prior to the deadline date for submission of your workbook, you will need to contact SET to let them know. You will be able to defer and currently there is no charge for this.

## Activity

*Check you have all the evidence you need from the previous bullet lists. Go to the* Critical Reflection *page of your workbook and scroll down until you see* Evidence for improvements in post-14 practice. *Read the text on the screen and then upload your evidence. You can add text to the box if you wish, and then choose* This item is now fully evidenced.

# Evidence of the impact on learner outcomes

You will need to evidence what impact the professional formation process has had on your learners' outcomes (i.e. what your learners are expected to achieve). To do this, you may find it useful to consider Bloom's (1956) *Taxonomy of Learning*. This section will help you to identify the evidence you can use, and will help you to set learner targets and to measure their progress. Taxonomies are stages of learning which occur in three domains:

- psychomotor (relating to skills)

- cognitive (relating to knowledge and understanding)

- affective (relating to attitudes).

The subject you teach might include all of Bloom's domains, or just one or two. Referring to them can help you see how your learners make progress and how your teaching has had an impact upon their learning. They are very similar to the Professional Standards which are in three areas and relate to:

- skills

- knowledge and understanding

- values and attributes.

## The psychomotor domain

The *psychomotor* domain relates to the skills development of the learner. The starting point is *imitation*, which could be watching a demonstration prior to attempting the skill, see Figure 7.1. For example, learning to ride a bike or a horse requires psychomotor skills. A learner studying bricklaying will need to learn to *manipulate* the tools prior to physically using them to complete a task. The final stage of *naturalisation* enables learners to carry out tasks competently. Learners will need to develop the required physical skills with your support.

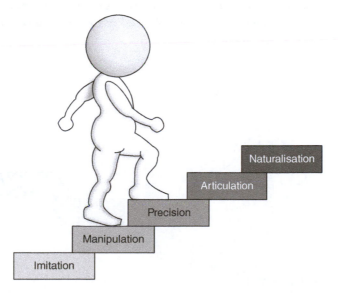

**Figure 8.1 Psychomotor domain**

Evidence (which should be anonymised) to demonstrate your learners' progress towards skills could include:

- an observation report of a learner's progress

- assessment records (formative and summative)

- case studies

- course reviews and evaluations

- individual learning plans

- learner feedback

- proof of collaboration and class participation activities

- test results

- tracking of progress against criteria.

The Professional Standards which relate to skills are numbered 13 to 20.

## The cognitive domain

The *cognitive* domain relates to the knowledge and understanding a learner needs to acquire. The starting point is *knowledge* which could be by remembering and stating what they have been told, see Figure 8.2. If your learners are undertaking an animal management programme, they may have some *knowledge* of how to feed an animal, but they may not *comprehend* why different diets are important. For example, feeding certain foods to particular animals may be appropriate in different environments to meet welfare requirements. A learner studying level 2 maths is required to not only answer the question correctly, but to also show the working out of how they got to their answer, which demonstrates their understanding. The final stage of *evaluation* enables the learner to evaluate what they have done with a view to improvement. Learners will need to develop the required knowledge and understanding with your support.

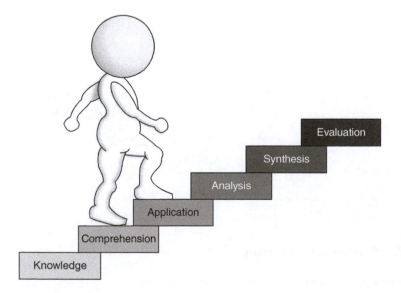

**Figure 8.2  Cognitive domain**

Evidence (which should be anonymised) to demonstrate your learners' progress towards knowledge and understanding could include:

- an observation report of a learner's progress

- assessment data

- case studies

- course reviews and evaluations

- individual learning plans

- learner feedback

- learner self-assessment

- test results

- tracking of progress against criteria.

The Professional Standards which relate to knowledge and understanding are numbered 7 to 12.

## The affective domain

The *affective* domain relates to the attitudes a learner needs to acquire, such as feelings, emotions and behaviours. The starting point is an awareness and willingness to *receive* information, see Figure 8.3. For example, when a group of learners first meet, they have to learn to listen to each other and take turns when speaking. As they progress, they learn to have the right attitudes and behaviours towards communicating with others, *responding* and *valuing* each other's opinions, for example, to actively promote British Values. The final stage of *characterising* enables the learner to demonstrate what they have done with a view to improvement. Learners will need to develop the required affective attitudes and behaviours with yoursupport.

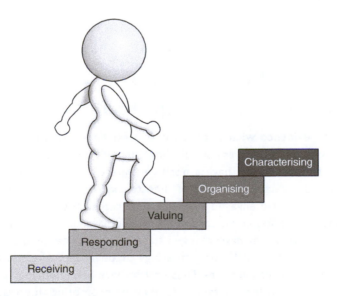

**Figure 8.3 Affective domain**

Evidence (which should be anonymised) to demonstrate your learners' progress towards attitudes and behaviour could include:

- an observation report of a learner's progress

- attendance and punctuality records

- case studies

- class participation activities, e.g. British Values

- course reviews and evaluations

- individual learning plans

- learner feedback and surveys

- tracking of progress against individual targets.

The Professional Standards which relate to values and attributes are numbered 1 to 6.

### Activity

*Look back at the previous three bullet lists to see what evidence you could use in support of the impact on learner outcomes. You might have other documents which are not listed, which is fine. Make sure you know where to access them and then go to the* Evidence of the impact on learner outcomes *area in the* Critical Reflection *section of your workbook. Upload your evidence to your workbook as before. You can add text to the box if you wish, and then choose* This item is now fully evidenced.

# Evidence of the impact of your professional formation on your organisation

You will need to evidence what impact the professional formation process has had on your organisation. The process should have helped you to develop as a confident practitioner, which in turn will have a positive impact on your organisation. Perhaps you have dedicated substantial periods of time to expanding and deepening your subject specialist area, or have engaged in educational research to improve your learners' experiences and results. You could consider how you have shared this information with colleagues and how they may have changed their own practice for the better. You may have been involved in standardisation meetings or been part of cross-curriculum or departmental improvement initiatives. These might have benefited your organisation by forging improved relationships, obtaining funding or promoting the products and services offered.

Examples showing a positive impact on your organisation could include evidence of:

- a case study of a learner who has made exceptional progress which can be used as positive publicity for your organisation

- a course review or self-assessment review which demonstrates improved retention, pass rates and overall achievement

- anonymised documents relating to coaching, mentoring and supporting colleagues

- changes to policies and/or procedures, for example, introducing a peer support programme

- developing links with external organisations, agencies and people such as employers or stakeholders to be able to support learners, or to enable staff to update their industry skills (e.g. work placements)

- external quality assurance reports which reflect how your work has impacted in a positive way upon the organisation

- improved working practices for learners with special educational needs

- lesson plans showing collaboration with colleagues, i.e. team teaching

- minutes from meetings demonstrating the sharing of best practice with colleagues

- records of standardisation which promote consistency of practice

- revised observation practices for teaching, learning and assessment.

## Activity

*Look back at the previous bullet list to see what evidence you could use in support of the impact of your professional formation on your organisation. You might have other documents which are not listed, which is fine. Make sure you know where to access them and then go to the* Evidence of the impact of your professional formation on your organisation *area in the* Critical Reflection *section of your workbook. Upload your evidence to your workbook as before. You can add text to the box if you wish, and then choose* This item is now fully evidenced.

*Tick the box at the end of the page to* Mark page as complete *(once you are sure it is all completed).*

# Summary

This chapter has explored how to complete the sixth stage of your workbook. This included how to evidence the impact of undertaking the professional formation process on your own practice, and that of your learners and your organisation.

**This chapter has covered the following topics:**

- Reflective account

- Evidence for improvements in post-14 practice

- Evidence of the impact on learner outcomes

- Evidence of the impact of your professional formation on your organisation

You might like to carry out further research by accessing the books and websites listed at the end of this chapter.

# References and further information

Bassot, B. (2015) *The Reflective Practice Guide: An Interdisciplinary Approach to Critical Reflection.* London: Routledge.

Bloom, B. S. (1956) *Taxonomy of Educational Objectives: The Classification of Educational Goals.* New York: McKay.

Brookfield, S. D. (2017) *Becoming a Critically Reflective Teacher.* San Francisco: Jossey Bass.

Gregson, M. and Hillier, Y. (2015) *Reflective Teaching in Further, Adult and Vocational Education.* London: Bloomsbury.

Roffey-Barentsen, J. and Malthouse, R. (2013) *Reflective Practice in Education and Training* (2nd edition). London: Learning Matters.

Rushton, I. and Suter, M. (2012) *Reflective Practice for Teaching in Lifelong Learning.* Maidenhead: OU Press.

Sellars, M. (2017) *Reflective Practice for Teachers.* London: SAGE.

Sullivan, B. (2016) *Introduction to Critical Reflection and Action for Teacher Researchers.* London: Routledge.

# Websites

Ofsted Teaching, Learning and Assessment in Further Education and Skills – What Works and Why (2014) – http://tinyurl.com/pf52qlx

QTLS Professional Standards Research Map – https://tinyurl.com/ycx93mw5

Reading list for Reflection and CPD – https://tinyurl.com/y9q9eh5j

Self-evaluation – https://tinyurl.com/k6stxhb

# 9
# Final action plan

**Introduction**

This chapter will assist you in completing the final stages of your workbook by asking you to work through various activities.

It will help you to complete a final action plan which will include details of the professional development you plan to undertake during the next 6–12 months.

It will also guide you how to share your workbook with your supporter and the Society for Education and Training (SET).

**This chapter will cover the following topics:**

- Final action plan a) key strengths
- Final action plan b) key areas for development in the next 6–12 months
- Next steps
- Professional discussion – final
- Sharing your workbook with SET

# Final action plan

## a) key strengths

The final action plan is the next section of the workbook which you can begin to complete when you are ready. It is in two parts (a and b) and requires you to identify the following:

a.  three key strengths which you have demonstrated during the professional formation process

b.  three key areas for development in the next 6–12 months.

The word *key* denotes that something has importance and/or significance, so choose things which you feel meet this criteria.

To help you identify your key strengths, you should look back at the following:

*   your self-assessment results

*   your observation reports

*   feedback from managers, peers and learners

*   professional discussion documents, and any other feedback, perhaps from appraisals and/or one-to-one discussions with colleagues or your supporter.

This will help you to reflect on what has influenced and motivated you, and which aspects of being a teacher you really enjoy and feel you excel at. Look for trends in the feedback you have received and consider what you have been praised for. You may have improved whilst undertaking the professional formation process. For example, what was originally an area for development has now become a strength.

### Activity

*Look at your documents, such as those in the previous bullet list, to help you identify your key strengths. You can view them via your workbook or open them if you saved them to your device. Make a few notes regarding your strengths, either on paper or by using a word processor. These will help you complete the next section of your workbook.*

The final action plan *part a* is an open invitation for you to identify and celebrate your skills and accomplishments which you have achieved during the professional formation process.

### Example

*Through the self-assessment process, Jalil scored himself 6 points for consistently achieving high levels of engagement and motivation with his learners.*

*He identified that he maintained high expectations of all his leaners when teaching his subject. Jalil's observation records supported this and praised him for inspirational delivery; raising individuals' aspirations; using up-to-date subject knowledge which is applied consistently; and having an excellent rapport with his learners. Feedback from learners identified how Jalil motivated and engaged them in his subject and how they felt confident to ask questions if they didn't understand something. Jalil's manager, through the appraisal process, recognised that he made very good use of non-verbal behaviours to build rapport and empathy with learners and colleagues.*

*Therefore, Jalil identified three of his key strengths as:*

* *I have an excellent rapport with learners which I use to motivate and engage them during the learning process, and I raise learners' aspirations.*

* *I routinely collaborate with learners and colleagues to support all learners to work towards their achievement.*

* *I use a wide range of approaches to ensure that all learners are consistently and appropriately challenged to a high level, and are supported and inspired to make excellent progress in their learning and beyond.*

This example shows how looking back at your self-assessment and other relevant documents can help identify your three key strengths.

## Activity

*Log into* My QTLS *and click onto the* Final Action Plan *tab in your workbook. Read the notes on screen and then scroll down until you see* Final Action Plan a) What are three key strengths I have demonstrated during professional formation?

*Key in the three key strengths you have identified into the* 1, 2 *and* 3 *areas of your workbook.*

# Final action plan

## b) key areas for development

The final action plan *part b* is focused on key areas for your development over the next 6–12 months. These should link to any themes you have identified throughout the professional formation process which have not yet been improved, or which require further progress to enable them to become a strength. There may be areas for development which you have identified through feedback from your peers and learners, or by reading and research which you have undertaken during the professional formation process, which you would like to expand on.

The final action plan *part b* should be completed to identify *three short, medium and long-term* activities that you will undertake in the *next 6–12 months* and should be cross-referenced to the Professional Standards (as in Appendix 1).

## Example

*Akeno chose to focus his professional development plan on classroom management. This included planning and delivery, assessment and updating his specialist subject knowledge through a range of activities. Throughout the self-assessment process, Akeno identified that another area for development was building positive and collaborative relationships with colleagues and learners to improve attendance. He was keen to continue to observe his peers to improve his own practice, and he wanted to formalise the sharing of best practice sessions across his organisation. Akeno also identified, through the research he had undertaken as part of his continuing professional development (CPD), that although he engaged in educational research relevant to his subject specialism, he had not spent any time with employers to understand fully their needs and requirements.*

Table 9.1 is an example of Akeno's key areas for development which is cross-referenced to the Professional Standards (PS). The specific areas he has chosen to develop are: Learner Voice; Sharing Best Practice; and Employer Links.

**Table 9.1 Example of key areas for Akeno's development**

|  | Professional Standard and specific area for development | Action to be taken (e.g. meeting with colleagues, peer observation, CPD event, visit to employer, research or professional reading) | Anticipated impact on learners (e.g. what difference will the outcomes of this action make to your learners?) | Expected date this will be completed by |
|---|---|---|---|---|
| 1 *(short term)* | **Learner Voice** PS 13. Motivate and inspire learners to promote achievement and develop their skills to enable progression | Learners to complete short survey in class to identify relevant enrichment activities to further develop their skills | Increased motivation and engagement, leading to more progression opportunities | July 20** *Date for completion to be within 1–3 months of starting the plan* |

| | Professional Standard and specific area for development | Action to be taken (e.g. meeting with colleagues, peer observation, CPD event, visit to employer, research or professional reading) | Anticipated impact on learners (e.g. what difference will the outcomes of this action make to your learners?) | Expected date this will be completed by |
|---|---|---|---|---|
| **2** *(medium term)* | **Sharing best practice** PS 6. Build positive and collaborative relationships with colleagues and learners. PS 10. Evaluate your practice with others and assess its impact on learning | Agree process with colleagues to enable peer observation and feedback – minimum of 3 observations per year per teacher | Improved delivery and assessment approaches will engage learners and impact on learner attendance to meet a minimum of 98% | Sep 20** *Date for completion to be within 3–6 months of starting the plan* |
| **3** *(long term)* | **Employer links** PS 20. Contribute to organisational development and quality improvement through collaboration with others | Arrange an annual employer forum to capture industry updates and requirements. Contact local employers to arrange work placements for learners | Learners to use the latest techniques and technologies to increase employability. Positive destinations and progression will improve by 85% | Feb 20** *Date for completion to be within 6–12 months of starting the plan* |

## Activity

*Scroll down until you see Final Action Plan b) What are three key areas for development in the next 6–12 months? Read the four headings, which are the same as in Table 9.1. Think about your three key areas for development and make a few notes, either on paper or by using a word processor. You can then key in your text in the columns in lines 1, 2 and 3, as in Figure 9.1. If you state a month in the final column, make sure you add the year too (one has not been added here to future proof the book).*

b) What are three key areas for development in the next 6-12 months?

| | | Professional Standard and specific area for development | Action to be taken (e.g. meeting with colleagues, peer observation, CPD event, visit to employer, research or professional reading) | Anticipated impact on learners (e.g. what difference will the outcomes of this action make to your learners?) | Expected date this will be completed by |
|---|---|---|---|---|---|
| 1 | | **Learner Voice**<br><br>PS 13. Motivate and inspire learners to promote achievement and develop their skills to enable progression | Learners to complete short survey in class to identify relevant enrichment activities to further develop their skills | Increased motivation and engagement, leading to more progression opportunities | July 20** |
| 2 | | **Sharing best practice**<br><br>PS 6. Build positive and | Agree process with colleagues to enable peer observation and | Improved delivery and assessment approaches will engage learners and | September 20** |

**Figure 9.1  Areas for development: action plan**

You might like to keep a copy of your action plan so that you can work towards it after you have completed the professional formation process. If you right click on it, you will be able to print it.

# Next steps

The term *Next steps* has been a focus within the further education and skills sector for several years. When a learner first commences at an organisation they will receive initial advice and guidance (IAG) with a focus on whether the course/programme they are interested in will meet their *final destination plan*. For example, a learner may attend a course to support them to gain promotion within their current job role, or a learner may wish to totally reskill into a different area of employment altogether. Alternatively, a younger learner who hasn't yet been employed will be starting a course to gain the skills, knowledge and understanding required to work in their industry of choice. An individual learning plan (ILP) will be agreed with each learner which includes their ultimate aim. This is known as the *final destination*. The term *next steps* is used to identify what actions need to be put in place to support the learner to get to their *final destination*. For some learners this will be progressing into higher levels of learning. For others it will be going directly into employment after completing their course and achieving their aim. For an apprentice it will be by achieving the apprenticeship standard and remaining in employment.

Measures are made by Ofsted regarding how well learners are supported towards their final destination through the four key judgement areas of:

- effectiveness of leadership and management

- quality of teaching, learning and assessment

- personal development, behaviour and welfare

- outcomes for learners.

If you are inspected by Ofsted, this information will impact on your organisation's overall grade. In addition, audits are undertaken by the government to check the overall positive destination data, which impacts on how much an organisation can access funding. Learner satisfaction surveys are undertaken by the government annually and *next steps* is included as part of the questions.

Next steps in the professional formation process relates to your continuing professional development (CPD) and how you will further develop your own practice. Your next steps should link directly to the three key areas of development you have identified in your action plan. You are required to write 200 words in your workbook to address the following points:

- What will be your next step in order to continue to develop your practice?

- Who will support you with this?

- Why are you involving them and how will they support you? How will you involve colleagues in this process?

## Tip

*You might feel you would like to discuss your responses to these points with your supporter, or anyone at work who will be involved with your next steps.*

Your supporter could help you to plan your next steps as well as give you some valuable advice regarding how to involve your colleagues. Feedback from the last Ofsted report could also help (if applicable).

## Example

*My next steps are to undertake learning modules for maths and English, which I plan to carry out in April to ensure I remain current with my practice. In addition, I have been supported in maths by my organisation's lead maths tutor, who*

*(Continued)*

(Continued)

*has agreed to continue this for me, and to help other staff who lack confidence. I will undertake both Functional Skills maths and English Level 2 as my certificates are more than ten years old. I will continue to research and introduce adaptive learning computer technology to colleagues and learners. The peer observations so far have had a positive impact on my own delivery. The team have agreed to work together to formally embed peer assessment across the organisation. This is to improve delivery, with a planned impact of improved learner attendance and retention. I will encourage other staff to undertake the professional formation process as I can see the impact it has had on my own delivery, which is evidenced in learners' improved attendance and retention data. I have shared my experience with other managers who have started to disseminate the good practice into their own areas.*

This example shows how working towards the Functional Skills qualifications can help improve maths and English. It also shows who will provide support and how colleagues will be involved.

## Activity

*Think about your next steps and make a few notes, either on paper or by using a word processor. Then scroll down to the* Next Steps *area of the* Final Action Plan *tab. In no more than 200 words key in text to the box on the screen to describe:*

- *what will be your next steps in order to continue to develop your practice?*

- *who will support you with this?*

- *why are you involving them and how will they support you? How will you involve colleagues in this process?*

*You could use a word processor first (or equivalent software) and then copy and paste your text into the box on the screen when you are ready. Don't forget to save your work and/or make a backup copy, if you haven't already done so.*

# Professional discussion – final

The last part of the *Final Action Plan* section of your workbook is to have a professional discussion with your supporter. This is known as the *final professional discussion*, and you can use the same template you previously used for the *interim professional discussion*. You will need to arrange this well in advance, as your supporter might be quite busy, and you wouldn't want to miss the deadline for submission of your workbook. It's not mandatory to upload a copy of the template to your workbook; however, it helps to evidence the process.

*Contact your supporter and arrange a suitable date and time for the professional discussion meeting. Make sure you have completed your* **Final Action Plan part a)** *and* **part b)** *prior to the meeting.*

Your final professional discussion is an opportunity for you to reflect on the professional formation process and the impact of the CPD you have undertaken. You should take along evidence of the CPD activities you have undertaken and/or completed, as well as your observation reports and feedback (your assets). You could view these online via your workbook if you don't have hard copies, or share them via the *I want to* button in the top right-hand corner of your screen. You will be able to discuss the impact on your professional development and any changes you have made as a result. This meeting is the ideal time to discuss your next steps and to confirm your final action plan prior to sharing your workbook with SET (which is in the final section of your workbook).

**Tip**

*You can share your assets with your supporter (or anyone else) in advance of the meeting via your workbook. This will save you having to take evidence to the meeting and allows time for your supporter to read your work and plan their feedback. You can share your workbook at any time for informal feedback from your supporter, by clicking on the* I want to *button in the top right-hand corner of your screen. On the drop down menu, click* Share *and select* With people. *Then complete the details and click* Share asset.

The professional discussion is the closing opportunity for you to ask for advice and guidance regarding any aspects of your workbook which you may wish to improve or change.

**Activity**

*Partake in the professional discussion with your supporter and complete the professional discussion template. Make sure it is signed and dated. Save this to your device and then return to the* **Professional Discussion** *area in the* **Final Action Plan** *section of your workbook and upload it. You can add text to the box if you wish, and then choose* **This item is now fully evidenced.**

*Tick the box at the end of the page to* **Mark page as complete** *(once you are sure it is all completed).*

## Sharing your workbook with your supporter

Sharing your workbook with your supporter and SET are the last things you need to do in the professional formation process.

You will need to share your workbook with your supporter two weeks prior to the deadline date for submitting your workbook to SET.

## Activity

*If you can't remember the deadline date for submitting your workbook, have a look at the Stage 2 column in the Deadlines for each stage table at this link: https://tinyurl.com/ya5q46ez*

You will need to give your supporter enough time to look through your workbook and to answer a series of questions, known as the *supporting statement*. The questions might take about an hour to complete. You can't submit your workbook to SET until this has been done. If you didn't add your supporter to your workbook at the beginning of the professional formation process, you can do it now.

## Activity

*Click on the About You tab and scroll down the page until you see Your Supporter. Check your supporter's details are correct or add their details if you haven't already done so, then click Save.*

At this point, you might like to read through the text you have keyed into all the sections of your completed workbook. This is to check for any typing errors or anything you wish to edit. You could ask a colleague to read it for you in case they see something you hadn't noticed. You won't be able to go back and change anything once you have formally shared it.

## Activity

*Prior to sharing your workbook with your supporter, go through each of the sections of your workbook and check your text for typing errors, or for anything you would like to edit or update. Ensure you are confident you have completed all the evidence requirements fully.*

Once you have shared your workbook with your supporter, you can't make any changes to it. You could ask your supporter to look at your workbook informally prior to you formally submitting it to them. This way, you can make changes to the content should you need to. You can do so by following the instructions in the previous tip on page 133.

## Activity

*Make sure you have fully completed your workbook and uploaded evidence to all the sections. When you are ready to share your completed workbook with your supporter, go to the Sharing Your Workbook page and read the text on the screen. Tick the box at the end of the page to Mark page as complete. You can then click the Share with Supporter blue button at the bottom of the screen. If you have not completed all the pages, a message will inform you of this and you can go back and check all the pages to see what is incomplete.*

You should let your supporter know you have shared your workbook with them. This is to give them some notice that they will need to add their supporting statement (by responding to a series of questions which are in the next bullet list). They will receive an email from SET to let them know how to access it. If they don't do it fairly soon, it could prevent you from submitting your workbook by the deadline, which means it will not be reviewed by SET. You might like to advise your supporter to make a backup copy of the text they add (perhaps by copying and pasting it into a word processor) in case of any issues such as the loss of an internet connection.

## Tip

*If you have shared your workbook but you realise you still need to edit something, you can unshare it by clicking the unshare button at the bottom of the screen. This will reset your workbook back to edit mode. This means you can still make changes to the content. However, if your supporter has already added their statement and you click the unshare button, the statement will be lost, and your supporter will need to add it again. This is a good reason for asking them to make a backup copy.*

## Supporting statement

Your supporter will receive an email from SET with a link, which, when clicked, will take them to the supporting statement area of your workbook. You might like to check that they have received it, and remind them you can't submit your workbook to SET until they have completed it.

## Tip

*Your supporter can read guidance regarding their role and how to complete the supporting statement here: https://tinyurl.com/ybn7rd6s*

The supporting statement consists of a series of questions, which might take about an hour to complete. However, it might take your supporter much longer to read your text in your workbook and review your evidence.

There is no word-count limit on answering the questions; however, they should refer to the Professional Standards when responding. Your supporter will be able to review your workbook and add responses to the following questions:

- In what capacity or capacities have you known the applicant?

- How long have you known the applicant?

- What is your professional relationship to the applicant?

- Please explain how the applicant has developed their practice and subject knowledge during the professional formation process.

- Please explain the impact this has had on their practice, learner outcomes and organisation.

- Please comment on their particular strengths and attributes which the applicant brings to his or her professional practice and why you believe they should be awarded QTLS status.

- Please provide any suggestions for the future professional development of the applicant.

- Is there any further information regarding the applicant or their practice which you believe may be relevant for SET to take into account in determining their application, or which may have a bearing upon the suitability of the applicant to be granted QTLS or to appear on the professional status register?

Your supporter is required to tick a box to confirm and submit their statement and then click on *Save and support*. Once their statement has been submitted, you should receive an email from SET and you will be able to access their feedback by clicking on the blue button *View supporting statement* at the bottom of any workbook page, as in Figure 9.2.

## *Activity*

*Once you know that your supporter has uploaded their statement, go to any page of your workbook and click on the* View supporting statement *blue button at the bottom of the page. Read their statement and make notes to help you with your future development.*

Depending upon the type of internet browser you are using, you might be able to save and/or print your supporter's statement by right clicking on it.

You might find it useful to discuss the feedback with your supporter. For example, you might be unsure of something, or they might have given you some valuable advice which you need to clarify.

# Sharing your workbook with SET

You are now ready for the final aspect of the professional formation process which is to share your workbook with SET. This must be by the deadline date, otherwise it will not be reviewed. You must have received your supporter's feedback prior to doing this and you must have paid any outstanding professional formation fees. If you are unsure about how to pay, give SET a call on 0800 093 9111 or 020 3092 5001.

## Activity

*Share your workbook with SET by clicking on the Share with SET button at the bottom of the Sharing Your Workbook page.*

You will receive an email from SET to confirm you have submitted your workbook and you can now relax as you have completed your workbook.

## Tip

*If you are not ready to submit, a defer button will appear on your workbook next to the deadline date.*

## The end of the professional formation process

Congratulations, you have how completed the professional formation process. Once your workbook has been reviewed by SET, you will be notified of your result. This will be within six to eight weeks of the submission date.

You will also receive an email from SET regarding a survey which you can complete to give feedback regarding the professional formation process.

## Activity

*Once you have received an email from SET with your QTLS result, you can log back into your workbook. You will see STATUS: AWARDED (if you have been successful) and you will be able to access feedback by clicking on the blue button View feedback at the bottom of any workbook page, as in Figure 9.2.*

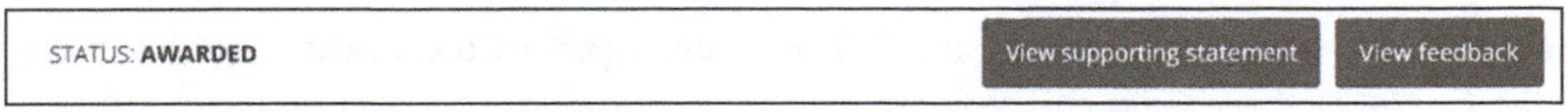

| STATUS: **AWARDED** | | View supporting statement | View feedback |
|---|---|---|---|

**Figure 9.2 Viewing your feedback**

If you have been awarded QTLS status, an electronic certificate will soon be accessible by clicking on the ▣◉◈ icon to the right of your screen, and then on the word *FEEDBACK*. Scroll down to the heading *CERTIFICATE* and click on the attachment called *Professional Formation QTLS Certificate*. You will then have the option to open or download the file. Once opened or saved, you can print a copy if you wish.

You will also receive a hard copy of your certificate in the post, normally around six weeks after you have received your result.

Achieving QTLS status demonstrates your professionalism as a teacher. It also demonstrates your expertise and experience to colleagues, employers and learners. However, it doesn't stop there. You will need to:

- maintain the currency of your QTLS and its legal parity with QTS by remaining a member of SET

- achieve the activities you set yourself in your action plan

- document your ongoing CPD

- demonstrate your commitment to the Professional Standards.

The final chapter of this book will help you with this.

After a short period of time, you will no longer have access to your workbook; therefore if you have not made a backup copy of any text or evidence you feel you might need, it's best to do it now.

## If QTLS is not awarded

If you have not been awarded QTLS status, you will be informed by SET in an email as to what additional evidence you need to provide in order to reapply. You can read your feedback by clicking on the *View feedback* button at the bottom of any workbook page. You can find out more about the review criteria by looking back to Chapter 2.

In order to reapply, you will need to click on the *Reapply* button which will unlock your workbook and give you access again. It will have been locked during the review and moderation process. You should then add the missing evidence and/or text on the appropriate pages. When complete, click on the *Share with SET* button at the bottom of the *Sharing Your Workbook* page.

You do not need to share it with your supporter again or gain another supporting statement.

You will need to email SET to advise it when your reapplication has been submitted at professional.formation@etfoundation.co.uk. Remember to include your membership number in your message.

The reapplication will be reviewed and SET will advise you of the outcome within three weeks. Currently there is no charge for this.

# Summary

This chapter has explored the final stages of the professional formation process, how to develop as a practitioner over the next 6–12 months, and how to share your workbook with your supporter and SET.

This chapter has covered the following topics:

- Final action plan a) key strengths

- Final action plan b) key areas for development in the next 6–12 months

- Next steps

- Professional discussion – final

- Sharing your workbook with SET

You might like to carry out further research by accessing the books and websites listed at the end of this chapter.

# References and further information

Gravells, A. (2017) *Principles and Practices of Teaching and Training*. London: SAGE/Learning Matters.

Petty, G. (2009) *Evidence-based Teaching: A Practical Approach* (2nd edition). Cheltenham: Nelson Thornes.

Scales, P., Pickering, J., Senior, L., Headley, K., Garner, P. and Boulton, H. (2011) *Continuing Professional Development in the Lifelong Learning Sector*. Maidenhead: OU Press.

Tummons, J. (2010) *Becoming a Professional Tutor* (2nd edition). Exeter: Learning Matters.

# Websites

Brilliant Teaching and Training in FE and Skills: A Guide to Effective CPD for Teachers, Trainers and Leaders – http://tinyurl.com/ocsef6o

Professional Standards for Teachers and Trainers – https://tinyurl.com/o2cv9fs

Guidelines for CPD – https://tinyurl.com/os92nqe

Ofsted Further Education and Skills Inspection Handbook (2018) – https://tinyurl.com/EdSkOf

Review of CPD – https://tinyurl.com/os92nqe

Reading list for reflection and CPD – https://tinyurl.com/y9q9eh5j

Society for Education and Training (SET) – https://set.et-foundation.co.uk

Society for Education and Training: CPD resources – https://tinyurl.com/y92lxqn2

# 10
# Maintaining your professionalism

**Introduction**

This chapter will explore how to maintain your professionalism now that you have completed the professional formation process.

It will help you to develop your practice in relation to the Professional Standards, and support you in planning your continuing professional development (CPD).

It will also give you an insight into progression routes for your future.

**This chapter will cover the following topics:**

- Motivation for excellence
- The Professional Standards revisited
- Progression
- Advanced Teacher Status
- My SET dashboard

# Motivation for excellence

Once you have successfully achieved QTLS status it is important that you continue your journey towards excellence. Teaching, learning and assessment practice is evolving at a fast rate and the best way to keep up with this is by having the drive, ambition and motivation for excellence. You should want to be an outstanding practitioner who is successful and consistent in their practice. This will lead to a positive impact upon your learners and your job role.

As information and learning technology develops, teaching, learning and assessment must also advance. You may have noticed that some learners progressing into further education are capable of holding a full conversation with someone, and be texting or using social media at the same time. Many young children are able to use mobile phones and social media, and yet there are some adults who don't yet use them. This can be a challenge if your learners are very competent using technology but you are not, or you are but your learners are not. You might even have a mixed group of learners, some of whom are better at using technology than others. Teachers can now use *blended* learning methods and *mix and match* techniques. This is about incorporating face-to-face delivery with training materials and learning resources across a range of communication and online networks. This can also include appropriate assessment tools to measure progress and the impact on learning.

## Activity

*What changes are currently taking place (regarding your subject, technology and/ or developments at work) which would motivate you to find out more about something? How could you go about fulfilling this so that it has an impact upon your learners and your job role?*

Keeping up to date regarding your subject specialism and teaching, learning and assessment approaches is all part of being a member of the Society for Education and Training (SET). It also demonstrates your abilities as a dual professional.

## Developing your practice

To keep your QTLS status active, you need to remain a member of SET and record your continuing professional development (CPD). You would have become a member prior to applying for the professional formation process. However, if you have let your membership lapse, so will your QTLS status. You will be notified by an email from SET when your membership is due for renewal and you can pay via direct debit to ensure it doesn't lapse. The advantages of being a SET member are stated in Chapter 1.

The most effective way of developing your practice is through CPD. This can be anything that you do that helps you to improve your practice and keep you up to date with your subject knowledge and skills.

For example, you might like to:

- carry out some relevant research relating to your specialist subject and then put the findings into practice

- read relevant journal articles, online reports or text books to try out new approaches with your learners

- collaborate and share good practice with your peers regarding innovative teaching, learning and assessment approaches.

### Tip

*If you are unsure of what CPD activities you could carry out, have a look at those listed in Chapter 6.*

As a member of SET, you can access its Online research library. This lets you view a wide range of national and international education research, allowing you to deepen your teaching and training expertise. See Chapter 7 for further information. You also have access to an online and hard copy of *inTuition*, SET's quarterly professional journal. This includes the latest sector and research news, as well as interesting articles and advice; book reviews; and details of events, training courses, meetings and webinars.

After you have achieved QTLS status, you still have access to the QTLS Professional Standards Research Map, where you can locate relevant resources relating to the Professional Standards at this link: https://tinyurl.com/ycx93mw5

The Education and Training Foundation (ETF) offers free and subsidised training opportunities to SET members via their *Foundation Online Learning* platform at http://www.foundationonline.org.uk/

Examples include:

- Prevent

- Leadership and management

- Teaching and learning

- Maths and English

- Special Educational Needs and Disability (SEND)

- Equality and Diversity

- Governance

- Future Apprenticeships

- Digital Skills.

You can also access over 7,000 resources to help with teaching, learning and assessment from the ETF Excellence Gateway at: https://www.excellencegateway.org.uk/

## Activity

*Take a look at the ETF Foundation Online Learning platform and the ETF Excellence Gateway resources at the previous links. See what's available to help you with your specialist subject and/or your job role.*

## The Professional Status Register

An advantage of being a member of SET is that you will be listed on its *Professional Status Register*. This is publicly available and shows people that you are an up-to-date experienced professional. You will be able to search for your own details, and other people such as future employers can view it to confirm your status. However, if your membership lapses, you will be removed from the register.

## Activity

*Take a look at the Professional Status Register at this link and check that you are listed on it. https://tinyurl.com/y7j4hlb4*

To remain on the professional status register you will need to:

- be a current member of SET

- have achieved QTLS status

- have remained in good standing by completing effective CPD annually

- adhere to the Code of Professional Practice (see Chapter 2).

## Activity

*Take a look at the Code of Professional Practice and supporting documents at this link: https://tinyurl.com/y8qavupy. Check that you are able to meet all of the requirements.*

# The Professional Standards revisited

You have been developing your practice towards the Professional Standards (see Appendix 1) throughout the professional formation process. However, it shouldn't stop there. As a professional teacher or trainer, you should continue to revisit them to demonstrate your commitment throughout your teaching career. Revisiting them regularly is the ideal way to plan your CPD activities and your future development.

## Activity

*If it's been a while since you looked at the Professional Standards, go to Appendix 1 and note how you are demonstrating your commitment to them.*

The Professional Standards relate to three areas:

- professional values and attributes
- professional knowledge and understanding
- professional skills.

## Professional values and attributes

There are six standards which are aimed at developing judgement of what works and does not work in your teaching and training.

This section of the Professional Standards encourages you to constantly and consistently reflect, evaluate and challenge your own practice, and the impact on those involved. They support you to be creative and innovative through your delivery, inspiring, motivating and raising the aspirations of your learners.

It's all about helping you to encompass values and promote cultural diversity, equality of opportunity and inclusion through your practice.

## Professional knowledge and understanding

There are six standards aimed at developing deep and critically informed knowledge and understanding in theory and practice.

This section of the Professional Standards requires you to focus on yourself in terms of your subject and/or vocational area, as well as keeping up to date regarding educational research. They enable you to develop and demonstrate evidence-based practice in teaching, learning and assessment. They also require you to collaborate with others and truly understand your roles and responsibilities, which will grow as you progress further in your career.

It's all about maintaining and updating your competence as a practitioner and a subject specialist.

## Professional skills

There are eight standards aimed at developing expertise and skills to ensure the best outcomes for your learners.

This section of the Professional Standards has a focus on developing learners' employability skills in terms of maths, English and the use of relevant technology. They also take account of inclusion and developing independent learning skills, allowing them to share responsibility for their own learning. There are clear links to collaboration with employers to maintain and update your own expertise and vocational skills. This involves contributing to quality improvement through collaboration with others within your own organisation. Another area for development is learner achievement and progression, and your contribution to this.

It's all about developing your expertise for the benefit of your learners.

## Activity

*Have a look at the Final Action Plan you created as part of Chapter 9. Make sure you demonstrate your commitment towards the Professional Standards by completing your CPD activities over time. Keep a record of what impact the activities have had on yourself, your organisation and your learners. You can update your plan at any time (keep a copy on your computer or device) and link it to your supporting evidence as you continue with your teaching career.*

# Progression

Once you have achieved QTLS status, there are various options open to you. You may decide you wish to progress into a different job role, apply for a promotion, or apply for a role at a different organisation. There are many roles within the FE and skills sector for people who hold QTLS status, for example: quality improvement, curriculum development, mentoring and management. You could also become an advanced practitioner and train and support new and existing staff.

SET has a dedicated section on their website called *Career Focus*. You will find lots of useful information there to support your career and help you progress further.

## Activity

*Take a look at Career Focus at this link and see what aspects can help you with your career: https://tinyurl.com/yaqv7puz*

# Advanced Teacher Status

In June 2017, the Education and Training Foundation (ETF) launched Advanced Teacher Status (ATS), which is underpinned by the Professional Standards. This is a badge of advanced professionalism and mastery in FE and training. ATS is a further step in improving and championing the quality of the sector's teaching and training profession through SET. It is a progression route from QTLS to a nationally recognised status that acknowledges enhanced professional expertise.

ATS recognises experienced professionals who can demonstrate:

- mastery in teaching and/or training

- an exemplary degree of subject knowledge in their area of professional expertise

- effectiveness in working collaboratively to improve teaching standards amongst their peers or within their organisation.

## Tip

*If you have any questions regarding ATS, you can look at SET's FAQs at this link: https://tinyurl.com/ycfq5gmj*

ATS is aimed at experienced teachers and trainers who have been qualified for four years or more and have held QTLS for at least one year. Applicants will have already developed and consistently demonstrated a high level of pedagogical and occupational/subject expertise.

Typically, the status is aimed at teachers/trainers in the following roles:

- teachers or trainers who are sharing their pedagogical/subject expertise through networking or coaching/mentoring others in their organisation

- practitioners with high-level technical and professional experience and/or academic knowledge of their subject

- advanced practitioners with high-level pedagogical skills in their vocational area

- curriculum managers or co-ordinators with a significant teaching or staff development role

- aspiring senior managers

- senior instructors, trainers and assessors and those supporting apprenticeship programmes.

Achievement of ATS will allow you to:

- demonstrate to employers and colleagues your mastery in teaching or training

- advance your career in terms of progressing to more senior roles

- use ATS as a designation in your signature and profiles.

Undertaking ATS is an excellent developmental opportunity that will enable you to:

- reflect on your practice to further improve your teaching and learning

- build collaborative relationships with colleagues and learners, developing skills in mentoring colleagues to bring about changes in their own and others' practice

- maintain and update your subject knowledge and educational research

- apply understanding of effective practice in teaching and learning

- critically evaluate practice and assess its impact

- collaborate with your employers, where applicable

- contribute to organisational development

- develop curriculum or teaching and learning leadership skills.

To be eligible to register for ATS, you will need to meet the following criteria:

- be a current member of SET and have completed a Declaration of Suitability

- have been awarded with QTLS or Qualified Teacher Status (QTS) at least one year before starting your portfolio

- have held your initial teacher education qualification for a minimum of four years prior to starting your portfolio

- be teaching or training in a post-14 setting (including training colleagues) for an average of eight hours a week (or equivalent annualised hours) for the duration of undertaking ATS. This could be in a range of settings, including: further education (FE) colleges, adult and community learning, work-based learning, employers, offender learning, armed services and schools. If you are teaching in a school, then your evidence must be drawn from teaching learners in years 10, 11 and above.

## Activity

*Find out more regarding ATS and how much it costs at this link: https://tinyurl.com/y83nx9kk*

## Teaching in a school

As a holder of QTLS status, you are legally entitled to work as a qualified teacher in a school (in England). You can be appointed to a permanent post in a state-maintained school and you will be paid on the qualified teachers' pay scale. You are not required to apply to the Teaching Agency for Qualified Teacher Status (QTS). QTLS holders are exempt from serving a statutory induction period in schools because they have already completed a period of teaching through the professional formation process. If you do apply for a position in a school, you may find each school has different application processes with different qualification and experience requirements. However, QTLS status is recognised in law as having parity with QTS. If you are or are thinking of teaching in a school where the headteacher is not aware of this, *Guidance for Headteachers* can be accessed at https://tinyurl.com/HeadteacherGuidance

## Activity

*Take a look at this SET webpage for information regarding QTLS and QTS: https://tinyurl.com/ybnz8mxy*

You will continue to be recognised as a qualified school teacher provided you remain a member of SET. Further details regarding QTS and QTLS from the government website can be found by following this link: https://tinyurl.com/o9xnzfx

# My SET dashboard

*My SET dashboard* acts as your own homepage regarding your personal information, CPD and professional development. It includes lots of information relating to you and your SET membership. When you log in to SET, you will need to click on *MY SET* (next to the *LOGOUT* button). Once you have accessed it, you will see menus and information as in Figure 10.1.

**Figure 10.1 My SET dashboard**

## Activity

*Log in to SET and click on* MY SET *(next to* LOGOUT*). Take a look at the information on the page, which relates to the following bullet list.*

- Member information – *your name and key membership details (to the right of the image).*

- Membership status – *your member grade and details regarding QTLS (in the middle of the screen).*

- Special interests digest – *your list of interests (below* Membership status*); if you haven't already selected any special interests, you can do so by clicking the* My special interests *link in the left-hand menu.*

- My professional development progress – *a summary of your progress in four areas, with a link to the more detailed* My professional development dashboard *(below* Special interests digest*).*

- News feed – *regularly updated news from SET, ETF and the sector (to the right of* Membership status*).*

You can click on the links in the menu to the left of the page, as in Figure 10.2, to access further information.

| My dashboard | CPD process overview | CPD activity 0 hrs |
|---|---|---|
| My professional development | Self-assessment | |
| My details | Professional development | ADD ACTIVITY |
| My qualifications | CPD record | |
| My employment | Reflection | |
| My programmes | | |
| My special interests | My professional development progress | |
| My mailings | | |
| | Self-assessment ☐ | |

**Figure 10.2  My SET Dashboard – My professional development link**

*My professional development*, as in Figure 10.2, links to the more detailed professional development dashboard. When you click on it, you will see further links which begin with *CPD process overview*. This is a resource to help you to engage with your professional development in an active and ongoing way. It should have an emphasis on professional discussions with your peers to support the development of your skills and knowledge.

This is a four-stage process which includes:

1.  *Self-assessment* – provides access to the self-assessment tool to assess yourself against the Professional Standards, as you did during your professional formation.

2.  *Professional development* (PD) – enables you to download a template to plan your objectives to meet your CPD activities.

3.  *CPD record* – shows how to keep track of your CPD, how many hours you have undertaken and how you have rated the activities. The number of hours will be generated from the information you provide when you add activities.

4.  *Reflection* – enables you to download a template ready for use regarding reflecting upon your CPD activities.

There are various other activities you can carry out via SET's dashboard. One of them is uploading information regarding your professional development. If you have completed some aspects of your *Final Action Plan* (as in the previous activity), you can upload details of these to *My SET dashboard*.

## Activity

*Access* **My SET dashboard** *and click on* **My professional development** *in the left-hand menu. Here you can add details of your CPD by clicking on* ADD ACTIVITY *to the right of the screen, as in Figure 10.3. You can now follow the instructions to add your details. When you have finished, click on* SAVE ACTIVITY. *Your* My SET dashboard *will now display the number of activities you have undertaken, as in Figure 10.3.*

If you wish, you can click on *EXPORT* to view all the information you have uploaded, and then scroll to the end of the page and click on *SAVE AS PDF* to save it to your own device.

| My dashboard | CPD process overview | **CPD activity 81.0 hrs** |
| My professional development | Self-assessment | Professional Formation towards QTLS 28 Feb 2018 |
| My details | Professional development | Prevent 13 Jun 2017 |
| My qualifications | CPD record | Ofsted Inspector Consultancy 12 Jun 2017 |
| My employment | Reflection | Verbal feedback, questioning and differentiation 02 Mar 2017 |
| My programmes | | |
| My special interests | **My professional development progress** | ADD ACTIVITY   EXPORT |
| My mailings | Self-assessment ⊙            ☑ | |
| | Professional development plan  ☑ | |
| | Activities            4 | |
| | Reflection            ☐ | |

**Figure 10.3  My SET dashboard – example of CPD activities**

There are lots of other headings in the menus in *My SET dashboard* which you can explore when you have the time. For example, keeping your personal, qualification and employment details up to date.

# Summary

This chapter has explored how to maintain your professionalism and develop your practice in relation to the Professional Standards. You should now be able to plan for your continuing professional development and have an insight into progression routes for your future.

There have been many external weblinks in this book to help you with the professional formation process. If you have found any which didn't work, please email sharronmansell@outlook.com. Also, if an instruction has changed regarding an activity which relates to the SET workbook, please do get in touch. This will help to update the book for future readers.

You might like to carry out further research by accessing the books and websites listed at the end of this chapter.

This chapter has covered the following topics:

- Motivation for excellence
- The Professional Standards revisited
- Progression
- Advanced Teacher Status
- My SET dashboard

# References and further information

Neary, S. (2016) *CPD for the Career Development Professional: A Handbook for Enhancing Practice*. Bath: Trotman.

Martyn, M. (2003) *The Hybrid Online Model: Good Practice*. Educause Quarterly: 18–23.

Saritepeci, M. and Cakir, H. (2015) The Effect of Blended Learning Environments on Student Motivation and Student Engagement: A Study on Social Studies Course. *Education and Science*, 40 (177).

Scales, P., Pickering, J., Senior, L., Headley, K., Garner, P. and Boulton, H. (2011) *Continuing Professional Development in the Lifelong Learning Sector*. Maidenhead: OU Press.

# Websites

Advanced Teacher Status (ATS) – https://tinyurl.com/yc7q7r3y

CPD information – http://www.anngravells.com/information/cpd

CPD text books – http://www.anngravells.com/reading-lists/reflection-and-cpd

ETF Excellence Gateway Resources – https://www.excellencegateway.org.uk/

ETF Foundation Online Learning Platform – http://www.foundationonline.org.uk/

Professional Status Register – **https://tinyurl.com/y7czqber**

Qualified Teacher Status (QTS) – **https://tinyurl.com/o9xnzfx**

SET Code of Professional Practice – **https://tinyurl.com/y79ffbvb**

SET Online research library – https://tinyurl.com/y9w27tjh

# Professional Standards for Teachers and Trainers in Education and Training in England (2014)

## Professional values and attributes

1. Reflect on what works best in your teaching and learning to meet the diverse needs of learners.

2. Evaluate and challenge your practice, values and beliefs.

3. Inspire, motivate and raise aspirations of learners through your enthusiasm and knowledge.

4. Be creative and innovative in selecting and adapting strategies to help learners to learn.

5. Value and promote social and cultural diversity, equality of opportunity and inclusion.

6. Build positive and collaborative relationships with colleagues and learners.

## Professional knowledge and understanding

7. Maintain and update knowledge of your subject and/or vocational area.

8. Maintain and update your knowledge of educational research to develop evidence-based practice.

9. Apply theoretical understanding of effective practice in teaching, learning and assessment drawing on research and other evidence.

10. Evaluate your practice with others and assess its impact on learning.

11. Manage and promote positive learner behaviour.

12. Understand the teaching and professional role and your responsibilities.

# Professional skills

13. Motivate and inspire learners to promote achievement and develop their skills to enable progression.

14. Plan and deliver effective learning programmes for diverse groups or individuals in a safe and inclusive environment.

15. Promote the benefits of technology and support learners in its use.

16. Address the mathematics and English needs of learners and work creatively to overcome individual barriers to learning.

17. Enable learners to share responsibility for their own learning and assessment, setting goals that stretch and challenge.

18. Apply appropriate and fair methods of assessment and provide constructive and timely feedback to support progression and achievement.

19. Maintain and update your teaching and training expertise and vocational skills through collaboration with employers.

20. Contribute to organisational development and quality improvement through collaboration with others.

https://tinyurl.com/ETFProfessionalStandards

# QTLS Mandatory evidence

| Workbook section | Evidence | Text |
|---|---|---|
| **About you** | Declaration of suitability (submitted prior to commencing your workbook). This must be noted as 'received' in the workbook (see Chapter 2 for details)<br><br>Your qualifications (clear copy images in colour):<br><br>1. Initial Teacher Education qualification (plus NARIC statement if gained overseas)<br>2. Maths and English qualifications at level 2 (plus NARIC statement if gained overseas)<br>3. Subject Specialist qualification (or CV) that summarises your work experience relevant to your vocational role<br>4. Maths and/or English qualifications at level 3 (if you teach maths, English or ESOL) | Your supporter's details (name and email) |
| **Role and responsibilities** | Your CV | Your journey into teaching (maximum 500 words)<br><br>Your current role and responsibilities, clearly stating the age range of your learners (must include post-14 practice, i.e. years 10, 11 and above and/or with adults) and subject/s taught (maximum 200 words)<br><br>Your motivation for undertaking QTLS (maximum 200 words) |

*(Continued)*

(Continued)

| Workbook section | Evidence | Text |
|---|---|---|
| **Self-assessment** | Copy of your self-assessment results (completed within the workbook) including reflective comments<br><br>An observation report (must include post-14 practice, i.e. years 10, 11 and above and/or with adults) of your teaching. This should be signed, dated and undertaken within one month following the date of registration. At least one observation must be from group teaching practice (five or more learners). The observation report will be the one used in your organisation. | n/a |
| **Professional development plan** | n/a | A summary of your development priorities, i.e. the areas of your practice that you have chosen to develop. This should focus on why you have decided to develop particular aspects of your practice. It should be informed by your self-assessment and first observation report (maximum 200 words)<br><br>Professional development plan (completed within the workbook). It must cover each of the three areas: Planning and Delivery; Assessment; Subject Specialist Knowledge/Skills. It should be linked to specific Professional Standards and be informed by your self-assessment and first observation (no word-count)<br><br>*There is the option to upload an initial professional discussion, but this is currently not mandatory.* |
| **CPD record** | CPD record of activities and professional reading which relate to the areas identified in your professional development plan (using the template provided in the workbook). The activities should be cross-referenced to the Professional Standards and the three areas of: Teaching and Learning (Planning and Delivery); Teaching and Learning (Assessment); Subject Specialist Knowledge.<br><br>Notes from your professional discussion with your supporter, signed and dated (using the template provided in the workbook) | n/a |

| Workbook section | Evidence | Text |
|---|---|---|
| **Critical reflection** | 1. Evidence from improvements in post-14 practice (i.e. years 10, 11 and above and/or with adults)<br><br>  a. An observation report of your teaching that demonstrates improvements in practice of the areas identified in your professional development plan (this should be signed, dated and carried out in the final month before submitting your completed workbook and at least three months after your first observation). At least one observation must be from group teaching practice (five or more learners). The observation report will be the one used in your organisation<br><br>  b. The lesson plan from the observed session. The lesson plan will be the one you normally use at your organisation<br><br>  c. Your reflections on how the lesson was received, including reference to learner feedback<br><br>2. Evidence of the impact on learner outcomes (e.g. written reference to improvements in knowledge; skills; attitudes; behaviour; and supporting evidence such as learner feedback and/or unit/course evaluations)<br><br>3. Evidence of the impact of professional formation on your organisation (e.g. development of links with other providers/agencies; contributions to organisation's quality improvement strategy; increase in cross-department working; establishment of a community of practice; minutes of meetings) | A reflective account of the professional development activities undertaken during the whole process of your professional formation application and an evaluation of the difference it has made to your post-14 practice, the outcomes of your learners and your organisation. The account should include a review of your progress and critical analysis of the different strategies or approaches you have implemented, with examples of what has changed with respect to your practice and learners during the process. You must also comment on how your reading of relevant theory and research has influenced these changes/developments (maximum 1,500 words) |
| **Final action plan** | n/a | Final action plan (completed within the workbook) identifying:<br><br>  a. three key strengths<br><br>  b. three key areas for development (short-, medium- and long-term targets)<br><br>A description of your next steps in order to continue to develop your practice (maximum 200 words)<br><br>*There is an option to upload a final professional discussion, but this is currently not mandatory* |

# INDEX

# GET SET FOR QTLS

## SOCIETY FOR EDUCATION & TRAINING

**Access to Qualified Teacher Learning and Skills (QTLS) status is exclusively available to eligible members of the Society for Education and Training (SET)**

For just £5.25* a month, SET membership gives you the recognition you deserve as an education professional, as well as:

member-only webinars and discounted CPD courses

networking opportunities via online communities on Facebook or local network meetings

progression from QTLS to Advanced Teacher Status (ATS)

connection to our online research library, blogs and articles from leading voices in the Further Education and Training Sector

keep up with sector news via your inTuition journal and e-newsletter

To find out more about the benefits of SET and join today visit: **set.etfoundation.co.uk/joinnow**

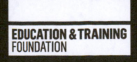

EDUCATION & TRAINING FOUNDATION

*Price correct as of 31 October 2018.